Lola Mae

A Life of Love and Learning

A Life of Love and Learning

Lola Mae Wilson Geisendorfer

Copyright © 2019 by Lola Mae Geisendorfer. All rights reserved.

Produced by Personal History Productions LLC

Helping companies, organizations, and individuals record their histories as a legacy for families, employees, customers, beneficiaries, and the public.

707.539.5559

www.personalhistoryproductions.com

Contents

Family Tree		viii
Introduction		xi
1	**My Beginnings**	1
	Mother's Early Years	3
	Father's Early Years	5
	Early Days of My Parents' Life Together	11
2	**Life on Clover Leaf Stock Farm**	13
	Our House on the Farm	14
	Father's Role	16
	Mother's Role	17
	Helping Out	19
	Ghost Story	20
	Expressing Her Love	21
	Airplane on Our Farm	21
	Two Younger Siblings	22
	Church and Social Activities	22
	Starting School	23
	Getting into Mischief	24
	The Radio	25
	Piano Lessons	25
	First Movie	26
	Christmas Programs	26
	Christmas Cookies	27
	Wintertime Fun	28

3 Moving to Round Lake, Minnesota — 29
    Our New House — 30
    School in Town — 32
    A Special Christmas — 33
    Church in Worthington — 34
    Girls Scouts and 4-H — 35
    Memories of My Siblings — 36
    A Close Call with Stan — 38
    Accident on Our Swing — 39
    A Second Movie — 40
    My Deepening Love of Reading — 41
    Relationships with Mother and Father — 41
    War Years — 42
    Graduating from High School — 43

4 Becoming a Teacher — 45
    Teaching in Country Schools — 46

5 Meeting Bob — 49
    Moving to Minneapolis — 52
    Teaching in Ocheyedan, Iowa — 55
    Ready for Marriage — 56
    Balancing Goals and Dreams — 57

6 Married Life — 59
    The Geisendorfer Family — 63
    Julie's Birth — 63
    Moving to Windom — 65
    Becky's Birth — 66
    Joel's Birth — 66

7 Raising the Children — 69
    Moving Back to Worthington — 70
    The Teen Years — 72
    Reflections on Motherhood — 74
    Family Vacations — 76
    Holiday Traditions — 77
    Losing Grandpa and Grandma Geisendorfer — 78
    Losing My Parents — 78

8	**Returning to College**	**81**
	Earning My Bachelor's Degree	83
9	**The Children Grow Up**	**85**
	Becoming Grandparents	87
	Moving to Forest City	90
10	**Losing Bob**	**93**
	Finding Faith	95
11	**Living on My Own**	**97**
	A Sampling of Lola's Homemade Christmas Cards	99
	Travels	104
	Actress for a Day	105
	Being a Great-Grandparent	106
	My Life Today	111
12	**Reflections**	**113**
13	**Afterword**	**115**
	Appendix: Geneva	**119**

Family Tree

SIMON JULIUS OLESON WILSON
b. Oct 7, 1846
Odense, Kommune, Syddanmark, Denmark
d. Jan 1927, Solvang, Santa Barbara, CA

JULIA JOHNSON
b. Nov 16, 1855
Stord Kommune, Hordaland fylke, Norway
d. Mar 4, 1892
Omaha, NE

JOHN CHRISTIAN PETERSON
b. Sept 17, 1857
Clayton City, IA
d. Oct 25, 1944
buried in Thompson, IA

THORA NELSON
b. May 29, 1857
Uvdal, Buskrud, Norway
d. Apr 11, 1896
Clayton Cty, IA

JACOB OLIVER WILSON
b. Nov 21, 1885
Laurens, Pocahontas, IA
d. May 27, 1968
Round Lake, Nobles, MN

ANNA GENEVA PETERSON
b. Mar 19, 1890
outside Clermont, IA
b. Dec 2, 1980
Worthington, MN

Lola's Siblings

JERALD OLIVER b. Mar 23, 1915, Buffalo Center, IA
THORA JULANE b. Feb 12, 1917, Buffalo Center, IA
WOODROW WARREN b. Mar 27, 1918, Buffalo Center, IA
CARMEN LILLIAN b. Apr 12, 1920 outside Granada, MN
ARTHUR GORDON b. July 7, 1922 outside Granada, MN
STANFORD JOEL b. Feb 23, 1924 outside Granada, MN
BARBARA ANN b. June 9, 1929 outside Granada, MN
DOUGLAS ALAN b. Apr 16, 1933 outside Granada, MN

LOLA MAE WILSON
b. Feb 16, 1926
outside Granada, MN
d. June 22, 2018
Worthington, MN

JULIE ANN GEISENDORFER
b. Nov 19, 1953, Worthington, MN
m. JOEL LORENZ

AARON LORENZ
b. Sept 26, 1979, Worthington, MN
m. ALEXIS WONGCHAOWART

LISA LORENZ
b. Sept 15, 1982, Worthington, MN
m. NATE HELLING

HARPER LORENZ
b. Apr 27, 2010, Ithaca, NY

JULIAN THOMAS LORENZ
b. Nov 22, 2014, Lincoln, NE

CALEB HELLING
b. Feb 4, 2014, Sioux Falls, SD

NICHOLAS LORENZ
b. Dec 27, 2012, Lincoln, NE

ARIS LORENZ
b. Nov 16, 2016, St Paul, MN

Family Tree

John Viet Geisendorfer
b. Feb 28, 1848
Ulsenheim, Germany
d. May 25, 1921
Waverly, Bremer, IA

Katherine Ihrig
b. Nov 1 (or 3), 1864
Falken-Gesaess, Germany
d. Nov 1, 1945
Los Angeles, CA

Thomas A. Johnson
b. July 27, 1859 (or 1857)
Norway
d. Feb 6, 1931
Brewster, MN

Martha Idso
b. Feb 1856
Norway
d. 1934
buried in Paullina, IA

Victor Henry Geisendorfer
b. Nov 16, 1889
Andrew, Jackson, IA
d. Sept 28, 1964
Nobles County, MN

Anne Bergine Johnson
b. Apr 11, 1895
Forest City, Winnebago, IA
d. July 27, 1982
Nobles County, MN

Robert Eugene Geisendorfer
b. Aug 6, 1927
Nobles County, MN
d. July 5, 1988
Brewster, Nobles, MN

Robert's Siblings
Marion Ruth Geisendorfer Navara
b. May 2, 1918, Brewster, MN
James Vernon Geisendorfer
b. Apr 29, 1929, Brewster, MN

Rebecca Jo Geisendorfer (Becky)
b. Aug 31, 1956, Windom, MN
m. Wayne Henkels (div)
M. Eric Sitarchuk

Joel Robert Geisendorfer
b. June 18, 1960, Windom, MN
m. Jill Bohning (div)
M. Shamese Rutherford

Nicole Marie Henkels
b. Aug 28, 1977
Minneapolis, MN
d. Dec 15, 2017
M. Edward McKenna

Robert Henkels
b. July 30, 1980
Minneapolis, MN

Theodore Henkels
b. Sept 26, 1987
Santa Rosa, CA

Ewan Patrick McKenna
b. May 12, 2010
Boulder, CO

Cara Elizabeth McKenna
b. May 8, 2013
Santa Rosa, CA

Anya Marie McKenna
b. May 22, 2015
Santa Rosa, CA

Introduction

As my mother, Lola Mae Geisendorfer, was approaching her 88th birthday on February 12, 2014, my daughter, Nikki, and I started thinking that it would be wonderful for her to tell her life story in a book similar to one that her own mother, Anna Geneva Wilson, had written about her life in her later years. We've always loved my grandmother's little book, and we believed it's helpful to know about the lives of the people in your family who came before you. Understanding your family's history helps you know who you are and better understand yourself. Nikki was running her own business, StoryTag, to help people organize their digital photos to tell family stories. She offered to design and produce the book for my mother once the manuscript was written.

To help my mother write the story of her long life, we turned to Susan Milstein from Personal History Productions LLC. Susan interviewed Mom over the phone over the course of several months. In those interviews, which typically lasted about two hours, Mom reminisced about her early years on Clover Leaf Stock Farm as the seventh of her parents' nine children. She talked about how sad her family was to lose the farm in the Depression and how they moved to a larger, but less desirable property in Round Lake, Minnesota. She described in great detail her elementary school antics and her early love of reading. She recounted experiences with her siblings, parents, and neighbors that left deep impressions on her and shaped her into the person she ultimately became.

Over the course of more than eight hours of interviews, Mom talked about her early days as a teacher in one-room country schools, how she met my dad, and how she raised me, my sister, Julie, and my brother, Joel. She talked about how excited she was to return to college and earn her bachelor's degree in her 40s. She recounted the sad memory of losing my father and explained how she went on as a single woman to create a productive life devoted to her artistic and intellectual pursuits, religious devotion, and church activities. Using the verbatim transcripts of the interviews with my mother, Susan created a first-person narrative, which my mother read closely and edited to her liking.

By the time that my mother's manuscript was completed, Nikki unfortunately was too ill from cancer to produce her grandmother's book. Tragically, she died at age 40 on December 15, 2017.

Although I was heartbroken after losing Nikki, I was determined to finish my mother's book, so I asked Susan to help me with the design and production.

Fortunately, my mother was still in good health and could help choose photos for her book. She passed away at age 92 after a brief illness on June 22, 2018, just as we were about to make our final choices about the design and layout of her book. My mother would have loved to have known that her book was completed and that her children, grandchildren, great-grandchildren, and future generations of her family will now be able to enjoy and appreciate her life story and benefit from the keen observations and insights she had to offer after many years of a life filled with love and learning.

Becky Sitarchuk
August 2018

Chapter One

My Beginnings

I was born on a gorgeous winter day. The sun was shining, the water was running, and it was just beautiful. It was February 16, 1926. I was my parents' seventh child, and my six brothers and sisters did not even know that my mother was expecting.

It must have been quite an easy birth for my mother. She knew that I was coming, so when the children went off to school, she washed clothes, hung them out on the line to dry, brought them in, and then called the midwife and the doctor. She did all that, and then I was born. My dad was away in St. Paul, purchasing cattle. Only my two-year-old brother, Stanford, was home with my mother. My older brothers and sisters went off to school that morning, and when they came home, my mother was lying in bed, holding me in her arms. They were so surprised! My eldest sister, Julane, wanted a baby sister, and she got one. The whole family always liked to repeat that story. Listening to them tell it, the story seemed so real to me that I almost could see it with my own eyes. That beautiful day, them coming home from school, and there I was—a baby sister. Number seven.

No name was put on my birth certificate because Mom and Dad at first couldn't agree on my name. My dad wanted to call me Lily, and my mom wanted to call me Lola. They compromised, and I was named Lola Mae. But even after they came to an agreement, they still did not add my name to my birth certificate. In fact, nothing was done until 1980, when my sister Julane and I went down to the courthouse in Fairmont, Minnesota, to add my given name to the official birth records.

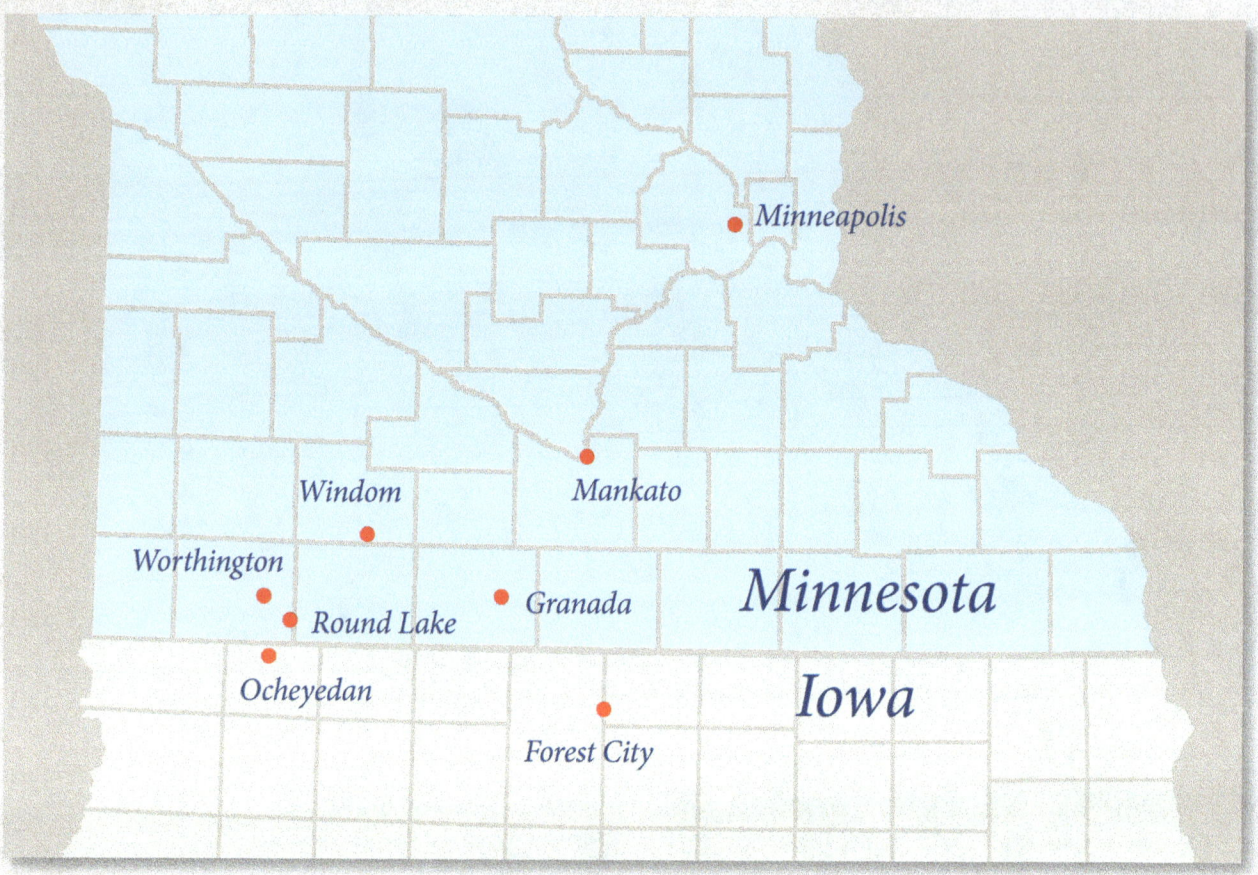

I was born on my family's farm, Clover Leaf Stock Farm, which was located out in the country, about a mile west of Granada, Minnesota. My parents, Jacob Oliver Wilson and Anna Geneva (née Peterson) Wilson, acquired Clover Leaf Stock Farm in 1920, six years before I was born, and we lived there for the first eight years of my life.

Granada was—and still is—a small rural town. Throughout the 1920s and 1930s, its population never grew beyond 400 people. The town had two churches: one was a Congregational church, and the other was a Methodist church, which we regularly attended. It had a grade school and a high school. Along Main Street were businesses offering everything basic that the population needed. Most little towns like ours had a hardware store and a post office. There'd be a restaurant, too, and probably a fuel station. But there wouldn't have been much more to Granada than that.

Mother's Early Years

My parents both grew up in Iowa, and, interestingly, my mother and my dad both lost their mothers when they were six years old. That type of loss shapes a child, when there's only one parent left with small children (and in my parents' cases, that happened to be their fathers). I would say losing their mothers at such a young age affected both my mother and father forever.

My mother, who went by the name Geneva, was born on March 19, 1890, just outside Clermont, Iowa, on a small farm on the Turkey River. She remembered that farm with fondness. Her parents were Thora (née Nelson) Peterson and John Christian Peterson. Mother was the youngest of four children, and she had a lot of affection for her older siblings. She had two older sisters, Bertina and Mary, and an older brother, Henry. Mother often shared loving memories of her gentle father, John. Her mother, Thora, died of pneumonia when my mother was a young girl. My mother's relatives were good to her after she lost her mother. She stayed with an aunt in Clermont until her father bought land near Forest City, Iowa, about 120 miles west of Clermont, and took my mother and her brother and sisters in a covered wagon to their new home.

Anna Geneva Peterson, age 21, in 1911.

Jacob Oliver (Jake) Wilson, age 26, in 1911.

In Forest City, Grandpa Peterson married again, in 1899, when my mother was about nine. Grandpa's second wife, Marie Jacobsen, brought a son, named Alfred, to the marriage, and then she and my grandfather had two children together, Florence and Joy. Joy was about the same age as my brother Jerald. Grandpa Peterson was the only one of my grandparents whom I got to know. He visited us from time to time with Marie and their children, and we would see them every summer at family reunions in Blue Earth, Minnesota. He was a great big tall man, very soft-spoken, and gentlemanly. A very kind man. My mother said he was a wonderful father. He died in 1944 at age 87 in Thompson, Iowa. Years later, when I lived in Forest City, I became a good friend of a woman called Mary Smith, who had worked as a hired girl for Grandpa Peterson. She remembered him as a quiet man who loved to read and as "the most wonderful man."

Geneva Peterson, on far right, with unknown woman and young girl (possibly an older sister and her child), 1913.

My mother told me that her mother, Thora, was a very plucky woman. My grandmother had emigrated from Norway as an infant. Her parents (my great-grandparents) had left Norway with their five children when my grandmother and her twin sister were just six weeks old. While they were en route to America, my great-grandfather died and was buried at sea. My great-grandmother had to come all the way to the United States all alone, a widow with five young children. When she arrived, she bought a farm near relatives in St. Olaf, Iowa, by the Mississippi River. She helped build her own house. She farmed the land herself and raised her children on her own. She never remarried. She lived on that farm for the rest of her life.

As a child, Mother went to a country school, and then she took some classes at Waldorf College in Forest City and earned a teaching certificate. She taught country school for several years before marrying my father. In my family all the girls—myself and my three sisters—followed my mother's example and became teachers. We didn't know anything else. We took it for granted that that's what we would do.

Father's Early Years

My father, whom everyone called Jake, was the son of two immigrants to the United States. His father, Simon (Sam) Julius Oleson Wilson, emigrated from Denmark, and his mother, Julia Johnson, emigrated from Norway. Julia lived with her family on a farm in Iowa near the small towns of Roland and Story City. She met my grandfather Sam there, and they fell in love. Norwegians didn't marry Danes in those days; it was frowned upon. But Sam and Julia got married anyway and went on to have four children: two daughters, Helen and Sophia Mattea (nicknamed Mattie), my father, Jacob Oliver (who was born in November 1885), and then another son, Julius Simon. At some point the family moved to Omaha, Nebraska. But they were living almost in poverty, and their house was cold. Grandmother Julia died during childbirth. After my father's mother died, his father, Grandpa Wilson, took his four children back to his wife's family in Iowa and said, "I cannot raise these kids by myself." He left my dad and his sisters and brother with

Simon Wilson, age 35, 1882.

Julia Wilson, age 26, 1882.

Great-Grandpa and Great-Grandma Johnson on their farm, and then he took off and went to California. He settled in the Danish city of Solvang and stayed there, working as a carpenter and helping out at a Lutheran church. So Dad was raised by his mother's family, the Johnsons. They took good care of him and gave him love.

Jacob Oliver Wilson, age two, 1887.

My Beginnings

Simon Wilson, as pictured on a postcard sent on July 31, 1913, from Los Angeles to his children in Iowa.

Reverse side of the postcard.

> Los Angeles Calif July 31 1913
>
> Dear Daughter Helen & children
> thought I would send you a picture of myself so you can see what I look like (Jake will get one also) I hope you & children are all well & prospering. I am feeling fair to midling. my Eyes are bothering me some now but hope they will be allright soon. I think I have caught a cold in them and then this glaring Sun in the daytime is hard on weak Eyes. Regard and love to your children and best wishes to you from your Father. S Wilson.

My dad and his brother and sisters started off working as hired girls and hired men. His sister Helen moved up near Forest City, Iowa, after she married Pete Helland. As a teenager, my dad made his way up to Forest City, working as a hired man. One day, when he was 16 years old, he was outside, working at his sister Helen's place, and he came in for morning coffee as he always did. There was a man sitting at the table, and Helen asked him, "Jake, do you know this man?" My dad replied, "No, I don't." Helen said, "This is your father." That's how my father met his own father again. Instead of getting angry at his father for leaving him, Dad developed a friendship with him, and he had that friendship until the day Grandpa Wilson died, in 1927. Since he died right before I was born, I never met Grandpa Wilson, but he left a gift for me—a small boat that he carved out of wood. He also built a violin out of a wooden shoe.

Jake Wilson, on far right, with two unknown young men, circa 1903.

The Wilson siblings, circa 1907. Top row: Sophia Mattea Johnson and Helen Helland. Bottom row: Jacob Oliver Wilson and Julius Simon Wilson.

The Wilsons. From left: Julius, Helen, Jacob (Jake), Simon, Sophia Mattea. Date unknown.

Simon Wilson with his granddaughter Julane Wilson, whom he nicknamed "Little Snoot," 1917.

Jake Wilson (on right) with unknown man, 1911.

Early Days of My Parents' Life Together

DAD WAS A WONDERFUL FIDDLER. The thing I remember most about my dad is his passion for music and the violin. Before he married my mother, Dad would go up to northern Iowa in the summer, when the weather was nice, and back to southern Iowa in the winter. When he came up near Forest City, Iowa, where Mother was living, he played for barn dances out in the country. Mother was a very strict woman; I don't think she went to dances. She considered my father a wild person because he played the fiddle at those barn dances, but she was infatuated with the dashing young man that he was. Mother remembered him having fancy buggies and horses. (He was always a lover of animals, my dad, and he particularly loved horses.) He had a charming personality that captured people. He had that charm his whole life. Mother was a quiet little country schoolteacher. They met through her sister Bertina's husband, Uncle Harry, who introduced them. They started going together in the summer, and things progressed from there.

At that point Dad didn't own his own farm; he was just a hired man. When they got married on June 14, 1914, he bought some farmland in Buffalo Center, Iowa, near Forest City. Dad was a hardworking man and a good farmer. Mom was hardworking and very organized. My parents' first three children were born on that farm: Jerald Oliver on March 23, 1915; Thora Julane (whom we always called Julane) on February 12, 1917; and Woodrow Warren on March 27, 1918. I don't know too much about that place.

Jake Wilson (above) and Geneva Wilson (left), 1911.

"I know what it is to be in need, and I know what it is to have plenty. I have learned the secret of being content in any and every situation."
Philippians 4:12

Chapter Two

LIFE ON CLOVER LEAF STOCK FARM

Jerald was five, Julane was three, and Woody was two when my family moved to Clover Leaf Stock Farm in 1920. That's where the next six children were born: Carmen Lillian on April 12, 1920; Arthur Gordon (Gordy) on July 7, 1922; Stanford Joel (Stan) on February 23, 1924; myself—Lola Mae—on February 16, 1926; Barbara Ann on June 9, 1929; and Douglas Alan on April 16, 1933.

Most mornings on the farm, we children would wake up to the sounds of my dad playing the violin. Then we would all come downstairs and eat breakfast in the kitchen. He liked to play fiddle music and songs of the World War I era and songs he had played for barn dances when he was young. I remember him playing the dance tune "Redwing" along with other dance tunes of the early twentieth century. Later he played hymns. He had a good ear. He could just hear a song, and he could play it. He played all kinds of music.

Mother would already have been up preparing breakfast. We had homemade oatmeal every day. We had our own cows, so we had rich cream. We had eggs from our chickens and some kind of meat, usually bacon, and we'd have potatoes and some type of fruit, sometimes from our own fruit trees. We often had grapefruit, which Mother and Dad had to buy. We'd often have canned fruit sauce, made from apples, peaches, or pears, that Mother would have canned herself. And Mom and Dad always

*Granada, Minnesota, 1923
(courtesy of Granada Historical Museum).*

drank a lot of coffee. (I never drank it as a child.) I don't remember everything about my childhood, but I do remember the good food we were brought up on. Good, healthy food.

Clover Leaf Stock Farm was a small farm. I don't know exactly how many acres it was. I know it wasn't a section, which is 640 acres. My mother wrote down 320 acres, but I don't think it was that large because when I go back and look at the farm, it looks more like 160 acres. The farm was at the end of a half-mile-long narrow lane that ran to the road toward Granada.

Dad raised hogs. He built a hog barn in 1920, and it is still standing to this day. In the summer he grew beets and sweet corn along with other crops. He raised the corn and the beets to sell to canning factories in either Blue Earth or Fairmont, Minnesota. He raised dairy cows, too. We had our own chickens. We had our own meat and milk. We had our own vegetables. Mother sewed all our clothes. We were a self-sufficient family.

There was a very neighborly group of people living around our farm at that time. The neighbors all lived quite close to each other; they weren't real far apart as you see in some Midwest farms. Our closest neighbor was maybe half a mile away.

Our House on the Farm

THE HOUSE WE LIVED IN on Clover Leaf Stock Farm was freshly built when my family moved there because the home of the farm's previous owner had been completely demolished in a fire. The new two-story house was lovely, but not real big for nine children. It had some beautiful colonnades that separated the kitchen from the rest of the rooms. The bedrooms upstairs were large, so there was space for all four of us girls to sleep together in one bedroom. The boys probably slept together in another bedroom upstairs, but I don't remember for sure. My younger sister, Barbara, who was born when I was three, started out sleeping with my folks downstairs, as babies and young children often do. But she later moved into the room with my sisters and me.

The house had built-in porches. They were a part of the house and had walls all around them, but we called them porches. They had been added to the house after it was built. We had a porch out back that the hired man used for his room. On the second floor above the lower porch, we had a sun porch that was real nice. The sun porch was open with no walls or ceiling, but it was attached to the rest of the house. That house had a lovely lawn, and Mother grew a lot of beautiful flowers.

Our home had no electricity and no modern conveniences at all. We had a wood-burning stove, and for fuel we burned either wood or dried corn cobs. The stove had a kind of reservoir that allowed us to keep some water warm all the time.

We got our drinking water from an outside well. We had a windmill on the farm that I think powered the water pump. We would have to fetch water from the well with a bucket and haul it inside. We also had a cistern outside to collect rainwater off the eaves of the house. We would use the water from the cistern—which was soft water—to wash up and bathe and to wash our clothes. We had a pump in the kitchen that we could use to pump water out of the cistern. We'd heat the water from the cistern on the stove for bathing. Of course we weren't allowed to take many baths because water was scarce. We got to wash our hair only once a week. It wasn't like today, where people bathe and shower every day, wash their heads every day, and have washers and dryers and all that.

Since we had no indoor plumbing, we used outside toilets. It sounds real primitive, doesn't it? If we had to go to the bathroom during the night, I imagine we used chamber pots. We probably went out to the toilet early in the evening, so we wouldn't have to be running outside during the night! It was cold out there!

We thought we were pretty lucky in Granada in those days when we got an icebox. We'd put ice in the top part of it, and the ice would keep things cool. We stored anything that was perishable inside it. All the canned goods didn't have to be refrigerated, and they were kept in a cool basement. The ice came from the lake and was stored in big icehouses in Fairmont, Minnesota, which was about nine miles west of Granada. Eventually, the ice house companies started delivering ice right to our house.

Because we didn't have electricity, when night fell we would use kerosene lamps for light. We also got something called an Aladdin lamp that was supposed to provide better lighting. I don't remember what time we would go to bed, but it was pretty early. Of course, when you work hard all day, you're about ready to go to bed when it gets dark. Farm life is just work oriented; you don't know anything else. That's the way it is.

It also was a different era. People in town might have had some conveniences we didn't have, like electricity and running water. We didn't get indoor plumbing or electricity until 1944, years after we had moved away from Clover Leaf Stock Farm to our next home, in Round Lake. And then, of course, when we finally got it, we really had a special feeling for it. We realized how wonderful it was. I hope these little details will give my grandchildren, great-grandchildren, and future generations a sense of what my life was like, because life has changed so much. And my parents changed with it. That's another remarkable thing: how they endured all of what they went through. Not just life on the farm but also World War I, the Great Depression, and World War II. They were survivors.

Father's Role

Dad was a hardworking man, and one thing I do remember—and this is really true—is that my dad loved the farm. He loved farming and the land. He grew quite a variety of crops on the land at that time. They farmed more varieties in those days than they do nowadays. In addition to beets and sweet corn, he grew alfalfa and oats—all the different grains. And of course he had the hogs and the cattle. Dad had chores to do off the farm, too, like going into town and getting things that he or the hired man might need. He was good at supervising the work that was being done. He had to oversee the hired man and then the seasonal workers from Mexico.

He always had a hired man who lived with us, ate with us, and did everything with us, just like a part of the family. This was usually a young man from the area around Granada. During the Depression years, from when I was maybe four years old until I was seven, my parents also brought in help from Mexico during the summer. There was turmoil in Mexico at that time. A family that had lost their money and everything they had in that turmoil came up from Mexico City to make money. They lived in a separate little house on my folks' farm. The man of the family helped my dad farm the beets and sweet corn, and the mother stayed in her house and did her housework. I remember Mother always said that when that family put their wash out on the line, their clothes were whiter than hers. My siblings and I would go up there and play with their children, and I would eat in their house with them. That's where I learned to eat Mexican food. I especially remember the homemade tortillas.

Some of the other Mexican families that came to help us on the farm over the years had older kids, not just small children. One of the families that came from Mexico City had a son who fell in love with my beautiful eldest sister, Julane. I don't know how old she was, but it was during her teenage years that this went on. He wanted to marry her and take her back down to Mexico City. Mother didn't want that, because Julane was too young, of course. So the young man didn't marry her.

Mother's Role

DURING THE DAY, MOTHER WAS mostly busy preparing meals for our family. We had homegrown everything—carrots, tomatoes, potatoes, beets, peas, cabbage, spinach, you name it. Everything that you can grow in a Midwest garden. We were brought up very healthily. Mother made wonderful pies with home-rendered lard, including apple pies. We didn't have an apple farm, but we had some apple trees. Some of our neighbors had nice apple trees, and we would get apples from them, too. Mother canned everything: apples, peaches, and pears that we bought, vegetables she harvested from her garden, and even meat (because we didn't have a meat locker).

She baked a pie almost every day: apple, sour cream raisin, cream pies—like coconut and banana cream. She baked homemade bread that you could never duplicate now. When she was older, people would beg her for her homemade bread. That wonderful homemade bread, oh, that bread!

Our family gathered together for breakfast, the noon meal, and supper. We always said grace before eating. We all sat together around a great big table that took up almost the whole kitchen. Mother prepared the food for all the meals: breakfast in the morning; then coffee for my dad and the hired man at 10 o'clock; then a big meal at noon with mashed potatoes, meat, gravy, vegetables, and pie. She used a lot of onions, and she fixed wonderful meats. Oh, she made wonderful steaks! She would prepare either beef, pork, or chicken. We would use meat from our hogs and cattle, and we had a lot of chickens. We didn't have the same thing every meal.

She made good fried chicken. Mother would catch a chicken from the yard, lay the chicken on a log, take a hatchet, and chop that head right off. That made quite an impression on me when I was a little girl. It was an awful thing to see—especially when that head would fly off and the headless chicken would still run and kind of jump around. But I didn't stand around and watch her. I know she did it, but it certainly wasn't a scene you'd want to sit and watch with all that blood. She was pretty brave! After she'd killed the chicken, she'd pluck off all its feathers, singe the skin, cut it up, and fry it. She did all that! Her fried chicken was wonderful, as long as you didn't think too much about what had gone on before.

In the afternoons, there would be coffee again, with maybe cake. After that, everyone would go their own ways and do their work, and then we would all gather again for supper. Supper usually was a lighter meal. If there was food left over from the noon meal, we might eat that. If we'd had roast beef for dinner, which is what we called the noontime meal, maybe we'd have sliced beef for supper. We'd also have maybe a dish of applesauce, because we had a lot of applesauce, or peach sauce. For dessert, there maybe would be a cake or pudding. We never ran out of food. Mother made sure of that. And Dad loved to eat. His favorite pie was sour cream raisin.

Our home was about a mile away from the railroad tracks, and hoboes sometimes came by looking for food. You see, this was during the Depression, and there were lots of unemployed men riding the rails and going place to place, looking for work. Mom fed them, but they ate outside on the steps. Probably she gave them slices of her homemade bread. When gypsies came by our farm in their big wagons, we would hurry into the house and peek at them through the windows. During those days we'd heard stories about gypsies, and we were afraid they might take us. They'd chase our chickens, take what they wanted, and leave. They only took chickens and probably eggs, too. Mother allowed that, as they did no other harm.

Mother was always busy working. Because there were so many children in our family and so much work to do, Mother often had a hired girl living with us. The girls she hired came from our neighborhood. They helped with the children, the washing, and all the different chores that needed to get done in a household.

Mother was a most efficient woman, so she found time in the afternoons, between preparing meals and cleaning and doing laundry, to sew and crochet. She had a big, old-fashioned sewing machine that worked real well. She made it go by pumping a pedal with her foot; she never got an electric sewing machine. It sounds like I lived in the 1800s, doesn't it?

Mother sewed all the clothes for all four of us girls. (She didn't make the boys' clothes. She probably ordered their clothes out of a catalog like *Montgomery Ward*. Or she might have gone shopping for their clothes.) We had very few clothes, but Mother did make special clothes for my sisters and me for school and special dresses for holidays. She didn't just sew for us; she would also embroider fancy patterns on our dresses. I remember my older sisters liked to dress up us younger girls; they'd put us in cute little clothes and pretend we were Little Red Riding Hood. When we grew older, we girls sewed some of our own clothes.

Mother also had to wash all the clothes with no automatic washing machine, just an old hand-run washing machine with an attached wringer, which she used until her elderly days. Washing was a process. She had to get water from the cistern, heat it on the stove, and then pour it into the washing machine. I imagine that's how it worked, because we didn't have electricity, but I don't remember exactly how that machine ran. She didn't have a clothes dryer; she had to hang all the clothes out on the line and bring them in when they were dry. During the wintertime, she would wait for a nice day to do the laundry. She'd hang all the clothes out on that day and bring them in before the weather turned again.

Think of all that she did each day! Of course, she did get exhausted. She said so later. But she was amazing! The women in those days were. There was a lot to do, and they stayed home and did it. They didn't go out, except occasionally to meetings with other ladies at church. They weren't running around town. They spent their days at home, working. That is what they were expected to do. Mother had to be an organized person.

Helping Out

M<small>Y TWO OLDER SISTERS HELPED</small> my mother in the house with the cooking and cleaning, and my older brothers helped my dad around the farm. My brothers would do everything that Dad needed to get done: milk the cows, run the machinery, and do everything that farmers do. They worked hard.

Since I was young during the years we lived on Clover Leaf Stock Farm, I wasn't expected to help my mother with the housework as my older sisters had to do. For the most part, I was free to do pretty much whatever I wanted to do, which was read a lot, draw a lot, and stay outside a lot.

The summer before I turned eight, my brother Stan and I were assigned the job of herding our cows in the ditches that ran beside the road along the west side of our property on Clover Leaf Stock Farm. We didn't have to herd them all summer long, only for a couple of weeks each summer during times when we didn't get any rain and the pastures were dry. The grass in those ditches was fresh and green, greener than the grass in the pasture, so the cattle would have something to eat if they grazed there. We must have taken the cattle to the ditches early in the summer, because I remember looking at the gorgeous wild roses that grew along the road next to those ditches. When I think back to my childhood on Clover Leaf Stock Farm, those beautiful wild roses are one thing I always remember. They were pink, but not just one shade of pink—many shades.

To get the cows moving up and down the ditches, Stan, who was two years older, would stand at one end of the road, and I would stand at the other end. After the cattle finished grazing near him, he would turn them toward me. When they finished on my end, I would send them to him. We would direct the cattle back and forth along this half-mile road. This way we would get the cattle to graze.

Since I was an outside girl, I ended up finding things to do to help my mother while I was outside. For instance, I helped Mother with the gardening: I planted flowers and weeded the beds. I also helped her with the chickens. I'd scatter feed on the ground, and they'd run and eat it. The chickens were allowed to run around our yard sometimes, but mostly they stayed in the chicken house. I'd gather their eggs. And in the spring, when Mother would buy the new little baby chicks from the hatchery, I would help her with them. I loved that.

On those occasions when I did help inside, my older sisters would often have me run errands for them: "Go upstairs, we need this." "Go downstairs, we need that." I didn't have big chores, but I would help out where help was needed. Mother also taught me as a very young girl how to bake bread and cakes, and I went on to win blue ribbons at the county fair for my white cake and bread.

Ghost Story

WE ALWAYS HAD A WHITE collie on our farm. My dad liked white collies, so he always ordered that breed from Chicago. The collies would come to us by train. Many things came by train in those days.

On Halloween night, people would drive down the long lane that ran from the road from Granada to our farm. From a distance, in the dark, they could see this white thing moving around on our farm. They couldn't tell that what they were seeing was our dog, and they believed it was a ghost. (Remember this is way back during those days when people were superstitious and believed in ghosts.)

Word spread through town that the Wilsons had a ghost on their farm.

Expressing Her Love

WE WERE READERS IN OUR family. My mother's father, Grandfather John Peterson, was highly intelligent and was often in the Waldorf College library, reading. He loved to read, and he passed that love on to my mother. My mother, in turn, passed it on to me. I didn't just develop my love of reading; I had it in my heart, passed down as an inheritance. I still avidly read books and magazines today. That started when I was a real little kid. My mother read Bible stories to me every single night for years and years. (The story of Joseph was my favorite.) I showed such a strong interest that she got special books, *Egermeier's Bible Story Books*, on a suggestion from the pastor, and she read all those Bible story books to me. I remember very clearly that she read to me alone—just me—so that was very special. My siblings also read a lot, but they didn't get that special reading time with Mother. She'd always say, "I'm getting this book for Lola." My mother was not overly demonstrative, but she showed me her love by reading to me. Now that I think about it, I think she gave me that special attention because she knew I wanted it.

She read to me before I fell asleep at night and sometimes in the kitchen, by the stove, while I perched on a stool. I don't remember all the details. I just remember the particular sweetness and tenderness of her reading to me.

My oldest sister, Julane, also read a lot to us younger children before we learned to read. And then, once we learned to read, we read our own books.

Airplane on Our Farm

During the late 1920s, it was quite the thing to have a small, private plane of your own. The Hodgeman brothers, whose parents owned the hardware store in Granada, had a little open airplane, and they asked my parents if they could keep it on a small piece of land down by our lane, a little ways from our house. My parents said yes, so they parked it there. My sisters were very excited about that and always wanted to get their pictures taken near that airplane. They thought it was special to have a plane near our house.

Two Younger Siblings

I was three and a half years old when my sister Barbara was born on June 9, 1929. After my birth, Mother had said, "I'm never going to have another kid at home." So Mother delivered Barbara at Hunt Hospital, in Fairmont, a town with a population of about 5,000, about nine miles from Granada.

The day that Barbara was born was called Children's Day at our church. I remember that day very well. It was a lovely summer day—the spirea bush was blooming, and my brothers and sisters were outside our house playing ball. I remember coming out of the house to play with the other kids, and my dad came to me and whispered in my ear, "Lola, I have a secret. You have a baby sister."

Four years later, on April 16, 1933, my youngest sibling, Douglas Alan, was born.

I remember when Doug was born, too. Of course, he was a tailender, and Mother had Barbara and me help out with him, just as Julane probably helped out with Barbara and me when we were young. Older sisters in those days had a lot of responsibility.

Mother would have me read to Doug in the kitchen, and he and I would play Parcheesi and Chinese Checkers and other board games. In winter, Barbara and I would take him sliding down the hills, and we'd play ball with him outside.

Church and Social Activities

My family attended the Methodist church in Granada. My parents were very faithful members who attended every Sunday morning, along with the older children.

One Sunday, shortly after Barbara was born, Dad was taking my older sisters and brothers to church while Mother stayed home with Barbara and me. I was outside playing in the gravel when I saw my father and the other kids leaving for church. I wanted to go along, but they said, "No, you can't. Not today." Well, they headed down the lane to church, and I decided, "I'm going to go! If they won't let me go, I'll go on my own!" I took off running down the lane from our farm toward the road that led to Granada. I suppose Mother saw me heading down the road and figured out where I was going. She called our friends, the Andersons, who lived about a block from the church. Before I made it to my destination, the Andersons came out to the road and grabbed me and brought me into their house for cookies and milk. Dad came by after church with the kids and picked me up. So I was a runaway for a day.

Once a month, on a weekday afternoon, Mother went to the Ladies' Aid Society at church. That was a big event for her, and that's where she met her friends. It was a social event for most women at that time. Since it was part of the church, I suppose they had Bible study, but they would also have lunch, talk, get acquainted, and enjoy each other's company.

Starting School

While we were living on Clover Leaf Stock Farm, we children went to a country school about two and a half miles west of our place. We referred to the school as District 80, I suppose, because that was the school district in which it was located. Since we lived in that district, that's where we all had to go. I attended that school for two years—for 1st and 2nd grades. I walked with my sisters and brothers (and the other neighborhood kids) all the way to school every day, year round, carrying a little tin lunch pail. It usually contained two slices of my mother's homemade bread, spread with peanut butter, and a cookie that Mother had made—maybe a plain sugar cookie or an oatmeal cookie—and an apple.

There were about 20 students in the entire school, and one teacher taught everyone in all the grades, 1st through 8th.

I was six years old when I entered 1st grade. On my very first day of school, the teacher, Mrs. Andress, met me at the schoolhouse door. She said, "Oh, Lola Mae, I'm so happy to see you!" And in my six-year-old mind I thought to myself, "I've never met her before. How does she know my name?" All day long, I kept thinking, "How does she know my name?" I was trying to figure that out. Of course now I know how she knew my name: all my sisters and brothers had been telling her that their younger sister Lola Mae was going to start school that fall, so of course she knew about me. And there were only two 1st graders that year, so there wouldn't have been too big a problem knowing who I was. There was only one classroom in that school, and I sat in the front of the other 1st grader, whose name was Roland Mayo.

In order to manage teaching everybody at the same time, Mrs. Andress relied on the brightest older students to tutor the younger children. My sister Julane was one of those older children whom the teachers picked to work with the students who needed help. She'd sit down and read with them. When I started school as a 1st grader, I already could read a little bit, though not real fluently. But I quickly started reading very well.

The children in the country school gathered together every spring for something called Play Day. I was not one of those children who was good in baseball or softball, but I found out early on that I had a natural ability to speak in front of people. In the spring of 2nd grade, I was chosen to deliver a reading at Play Day. My teacher chose the piece for me, and I still remember the first lines: "Do I like boys? I should say not. And then take my brother, Tom." I won a prize for my reading at Play Day that year. I wasn't afraid, and I enjoyed performing.

Getting into Mischief

THE 1ST- AND 2ND-GRADE KIDS were let out of school earlier each day than the older kids. We were pretty good kids, and usually we didn't get into any trouble—we didn't fight or anything like that to cause problems after school. I usually walked straight home by myself. And if I came upon any ferocious-looking dogs, I would drop down onto my hands and knees in the ditch that ran along the opposite side of the road, and I'd crawl past the dog so he wouldn't bother me.

After I finished 1st grade, our teacher, Mrs. Andress, moved to Blue Earth, and we got a new teacher, Mrs. Clemensen. One day, during 2nd grade, after we younger kids were dismissed, my friends and I climbed into Mrs. Clemensen's car and got into her makeup. Mrs. Clemensen drove eight miles each day from her home in Fairmont to Granada, and she'd park her car outside the schoolhouse. That afternoon, early in the fall, she'd left her car unlocked. Our teacher wore a lot of makeup, and we thought she was beautiful! In her car, we little 1st- and 2nd-grade girls put her makeup all over our faces—rouge, eye makeup, lipstick. We put it on heavy. Can't you just see those little girls with all that makeup on? We weren't really the kind to get into mischief, but we just got tempted that day. We left the car a mess, makeup all over the place. And what did we do after that? We ran home. We had to. While I was heading home that day, I was thinking that my mother was going to scold me, looking as I did. But you know, she never said anything. I didn't want to go back to school the next day. I thought the teacher would say something about what we girls had done, but she also never said a word about it. She must have known we had been in her car because we left it such a mess. After that, she always locked her car doors; we tried but we could never get in again.

The Radio

IN THE AFTERNOONS, I WOULD always hurry home from school so I could listen to Jack Armstrong. We had one of those big, fancy radios that occupied a big space in the corner of the living room. We would also listen to programs like *Lux Radio Theatre*. I used to love that program because you got a taste of the movies, which felt to me like another world. In the evenings, after supper was over and everything was all cleaned up, our whole family often sat together and listened to the radio. I used to wonder about how it worked. Where did that noise come from? It just fascinated me.

Piano Lessons

I'M VERY SORRY I NEVER learned to play the violin like my dad. He was so passionate about the violin, and he played it so well. Instead, we all took piano lessons. Mother played the piano, and she insisted that we all take lessons. Sometimes, one of us would accompany Father while he played the violin. While we were living on Clover Leaf Stock Farm, my older sisters, Julane and Carmen, took piano lessons from a woman in Granada named Mrs. Tesky. She was Mom's friend from the Methodist church, and she was very good. I didn't take lessons from her because I didn't start until I was in 5th grade, after we moved away from Granada. My sisters learned to play very well. Julane got so good that when she was only in the 7th grade, she played the piano at church services.

First Movie

When I was in the 3rd grade, right before we moved away from Clover Leaf Stock Farm, I was invited to the birthday party of a neighbor girl, Betty Wolters. Her parents took us to Fairmont to see the first movie that I ever saw in my life: Shirley Temple in *The Little Colonel*. That was very exciting! I can still picture the long lines in front of the theater waiting to see that movie. And then, because Barbara and I both wanted to look like Shirley Temple, Mom would take the curling iron and curl our hair like hers. We didn't actually look like her, but we thought we did.

That first movie was so special for me. Even after that, I saw movies rarely. In fact, I didn't see another movie until I got to the 7th grade. Whenever I'm in Fairmont and I go by that old movie theater, I still think about that first movie.

Christmas Programs

At Christmastime each year, we would have a program at our church in the evening. Mother was very creative, and she'd sew us girls really darling little jersey dresses every year for the holiday season. Some years she would make them in red jersey; other years she'd make them in bright green—always red or green and always alike. We'd wear them to the Christmas programs, probably with long underwear.

We'd also put on a Christmas program one afternoon each year in our country school. All the mothers of the students would attend the program; they would have lunch and socialize and exchange gifts with each other. It was a very friendly little community.

Each child in the country school would be given a piece to memorize and recite at the Christmas program, just cute stories about Christmas. I stood up and recited my first piece from memory when I was in the 1st grade and then again in the 2nd grade. Since I was just learning to read at that point, my sisters helped me memorize my pieces. I also recited those same pieces at the Christmas programs in our little Methodist church. I don't remember the specific pieces now, but they were maybe two pages long.

Many years later, Mother went to visit an old friend of hers from Granada named Dana Parker, who was in a nursing home. Both Mother and Dana were in their 80s by then, and they got into a conversation:

Dana said, "Geneva, I always remember one of your daughters from Sunday School delivering a piece in the Sunday School Christmas program. I remember that little girl so well, but I don't remember her name."

My mom said, "Was it Julane?" (My oldest sister was always in the spotlight.)

"No, it wasn't Julane."

"Was it Carmen?" Mom asked. "That's my second daughter."

"No, no. It wasn't Carmen."

And then Mother said, "Was it Barbara?" (She was my younger sister, and she was quite outstanding, too.)

"No, it wasn't Barbara," Dana said. "But you had another daughter, didn't you?"

Mother said, "Oh! Lola Mae!" (That's what they used to call me.)

And Dana said, "That's the one. That's the one. Oh, she was *so* good."

People have asked me, "What was it like to be the seventh out of nine? What was it like to be one of so many children?" I read once that when you grow up in a big family, you have to find your own identity. Maybe memorizing pieces and learning to deliver them in public was my way of carving out my own identity. Back then, I took it for granted. I never thought that's what I was doing, but maybe it was.

Christmas Cookies

ON CHRISTMAS EVE WE ALWAYS had oyster stew. Forever and ever, always oyster stew.

Oysters and cream—that's most of what is in oyster stew. I imagine my parents had to go to one of the grocery stores in Fairmont to find fresh oysters. But the cream we used came from our own dairy cows' milk.

About a half mile to the east of our property lived a family named the Tonnes. They had come from Germany after World War I, both the husband and wife. Mrs. Tonne made cookies that looked just like pictures I'd seen of those fancy, fancy German Christmas cookies—really highly decorated. Mrs. Tonne would hang all those cookies on her Christmas tree in the early part of December; they were her decorations. As a little girl, I would walk across the plowed field to the Tonnes' house, and I would look at those cookies hanging on the tree and admire them.

One day Mrs. Tonne said, "Well, Lola Mae, after Christmas you come on over here, and you and I will have a little party and eat some of those cookies with milk." In the weeks leading up to Christmas, I would go over there many times and look at those cookies, kind of hungering for them, and excited because I knew I was going to be able to eat them after Christmas. None of the other kids in my family wanted them. They thought they'd be dusty because they'd have been hanging there so long. Mother said she, too, wondered about that, but she allowed me to take Mrs. Tonne up on her invitation. So one day after Christmas, I walked again across that plowed field, and Mrs. Tonne and I sat by a window in her kitchen looking out over her yard and ate cookies and drank milk. (I drank milk; she probably drank coffee.) After that first time, I ended up going back again a couple of more years. I felt so special eating those beautiful cookies. I never could figure out why nobody else wanted them. "But, Lola," my sisters and brothers would say, "they're dusty!" I didn't care. They were wonderful! Now that I am older, I think of Mrs. Tonne and realize that she probably enjoyed herself, too.

Wintertime Fun

WINTERTIME AT CLOVER LEAF STOCK Farm was fun! We would have snowball fights, run around in the snow, and play snow games like fox and geese. We had sleds and went sliding down the hills around our place. I loved it!

Since it was so cold and we had a long ways to walk to school, we always wore long underwear in the winter. Come spring, we could hardly wait to get those itchy things off! Some of the other girls at school got to get their underwear off earlier than we did. I would say to Mom, "Why can't we get ours off as early as so-and-so?" And Mother would say, "I bet they get more colds than you do!"

Chapter Three

Moving to Round Lake, Minnesota

In 1934, my dad lost his farm in Granada. It was during the Depression, and he just couldn't make the payments on that farm anymore. He sat down and cried when he lost the land. My dad was a good farmer, and he kept his land up well. I really don't know why he ran into financial problems. I remember hearing rumors that neighbor people wanted our land. And then, after we moved away, those neighbors got ownership of our farm. I don't know anything more than that. That could have been what was going on, but I don't know all the details.

At the time, all I knew was that we were going to move, and I didn't want to move. Nobody did. My mother surely didn't. We loved the farm, and we had good friends around Granada. But it was something that we had to do. I know my dad felt terrible losing the farm, especially with nine kids. It was very rough on Mother and Dad. It was a difficult, trying time for all of us.

Dad had a banker friend in Fairmont named John Haekel. He also had quite a few children, and my siblings and I were friends with his children. This man trusted my dad. Through him, Dad was able to get a loan so he could buy land in Round Lake, Minnesota, about 65 miles west of Granada and close to the town of Worthington, where I live today. Dad bought a 640-acre farm with a lakebed on it. The new farm was much bigger than Clover Leaf Stock Farm, but it wasn't well kept. The lakebed was a concern because it was prone to flooding. When it rained, the lakebed might fill up with water and drown all the crops. Dad must have gotten a pretty good deal on that farm because of it.

Dad got enough money together to make a down payment on the land, and he made payments on that loan for many, many years. We bought the land in the fall of 1934, but we didn't move there until 1935. You just couldn't up and move there in the cold of winter, with the ice and the snow. We waited until March.

On his farm in Round Lake, Dad still raised sweet corn, which he would take to the canning factory in Fairmont. He also raised a variety of other crops: wheat, barley, and all the crops that people typically grow in southwestern Minnesota. My dad tilled the old lakebed, which hadn't been planted before, and he found that it had very good soil. He grew potatoes there, which he would sell to the Sather grocery store in Round Lake. He didn't have as much machinery as farmers do nowadays. He probably only had a threshing machine, a tractor, and a truck.

A large portion of the farm was pastureland. We were near Indian Lake, and an inlet of that lake extended onto our farm. In addition to dairy cows, my father raised stock cattle and hogs. The stock cattle were kept in a separate pasture that ran along the western side of our acreage. At night, they were kept in a barn that was separate from the barn for our dairy cows. Dad sold his stock cattle in Sioux City, Iowa.

Our New House

THERE WERE TWO HOUSES ON that 640-acre farm. One house was for the hired man and his family. The other was for our family. Our house was not in good shape when we moved in. It was a big, old house, and it needed a lot of care. It had been built in the early 1900s, long before we came there. It was a Sears Roebuck house; the store sent all the makings of a house to the original owner, and the owner built it. By the time we moved in, it had fallen into disrepair. The yard, especially, needed a lot of work. The house was surrounded by mud, right up to the front steps. And the house itself was not well insulated. In the winter, it was so cold inside that water froze in cups and glasses. We had to hurry and run downstairs in the morning to get warm.

Like our first house, this one had no central heating or indoor plumbing; we didn't get those conveniences until 1944. We depended on wood stoves to heat the entire house. There was one stove sitting in between the living room and the dining room, and then we had the kitchen stove. We would gather around it to warm up. If we wanted hot water for bathing or washing up, we had to heat the water on the stove, using cobs or wood for fuel. Taking a bath took a lot of effort, so we mostly took sponge baths.

Eventually, I grew very fond of that house. It had a lovely two-story floor plan with lots of room. Downstairs was a big kitchen, a big built-on porch, a dining room, a living room, and a bedroom—all very large! Upstairs, there were six bedrooms and a big attic. There was plenty of room for all eight of us, plus Mother and Father. (My oldest sister, Julane, did not move with us to Round Lake, because she was already teaching school by then.)

The house in Round Lake where Lola's family lived starting in 1935. Photo dated March 19, 1962.

One of the bedrooms upstairs was big enough to be the master bedroom for a husband and wife, but my two sisters, Carmen and Barbara, took that room. Mother and Dad slept upstairs at first, but they eventually moved to the downstairs bedroom. The boys were scattered around in other rooms.

I had a little bedroom of my own. I was the only child in the family who had a room to myself; all my brothers and sisters had to share theirs. I had a small iron bed that a pastor and his wife had given me when they left Granada. I always liked that little iron bed; it was so cute. It wasn't a baby bed; it was just a small, twin-sized sturdy bed. The room had a closet, too. My family called it the "Lola Mae room." Even the people who later bought the house always said, "And that was the 'Lola Mae room.'" I kept it until Carmen moved away, and then Barbara and I shared a room.

School in Town

I WAS IN 3RD GRADE when we moved to Round Lake, which means I was between eight and nine years old. Before we left our country school near Granada, the teacher gave us a party with homemade ice cream! This is still one of my favorite foods. We enrolled in a town school, and it was really quite an experience going from a country school to a school with a lot more students. Instead of one teacher for all the grades, we were split into different classes. I was placed in a combined class of 3rd and 4th graders, and there were about 20 of us in that class. Instead of walking to school for two and a half miles, we now took a bus. Delbert Coyer, the driver, waited patiently every day for the six Wilson kids to get on the bus.

By the time I was in 3rd grade, I was a good reader, and I had a lot of confidence in that area. One of the first things I did when I started school in Round Lake was to walk up to my new teacher, Miss Lundholm, and say, "Can I read out loud to the kids?" Imagine that! She later told me this was an unexpected request from this little country girl. I said, "I want to read *The Story of Dr. Dolittle* by Hugh Lofting to the kids." She said yes, and she put me on a stool in front of the class. Years later, she told me that she at first questioned if letting me read aloud was the right thing to do, because she had no idea if I could read or not. But once she heard me read, she thought to herself, "Wow!" She just couldn't believe how incredibly well I could read. I ended up reading the entire book to the 3rd- and 4th-grade class, a chapter a day. And I showed the pictures, too. It took a lot of nerve, when I think about it now.

I was a confident little girl in that way. I guess because I loved to read, I felt I had to share that love. I still feel that way. There's just something in me, driving me to share my love of the written word.

Although I was confident of my ability to read as a young girl, I wasn't confident in every way; for instance, I didn't think I looked very good in those days, and that affected my self-confidence. Mother combed my hair every day and dressed all of us well, but I think I looked a little scraggly. I was not good at sports. I wanted to be a good runner and a good ballplayer, but I was not. We used to choose kids to be on teams, and I just hated that! I was never chosen first because I couldn't play ball well. I was not confident when it came to social situations, either.

I was a shy little girl in many ways, but when it came to reading and performing, that's what I did well. And when it came to competing in a spelling bee, I was often first.

Because I was shy, it took me some time to get acquainted with people in my new school. Here I was, a little country girl coming into town. Back in my country school, I had known everyone, but coming to a strange school, it takes a while, and they look you over pretty good before they really relax about you and finally decide they want you. Then, once they accept you, you get in.

One of the first friends I met in that town school was Marie Waage Christianson, and she remained my friend for the rest of her life. Marie was in the 4th grade when I moved to Round Lake. Toward the end of her life, she was in a nursing home, and I would visit her there. We would remark to each other, "We've been friends for so many years!" Sadly, she died in 2017.

I liked almost all my teachers, but I especially liked the one I had that first year, in the combined 3rd- and 4th-grade class—Miss Lundholm. Then there was a 5th- and 6th-grade teacher—I don't want to even mention her name—who was very strict. She used to argue with my brother Stan about how many kids we had in our family. Stan said, "We have nine," and this teacher said, "No. You have 10." And Stan said, "No. We have nine. I should know how many kids are in my family." She wasn't our favorite teacher. Before I went to 5th grade, I was kind of nervous about going into her room; I'd heard about her being so strict. I used to like to draw on all my school papers, but this particular teacher would not allow that.

When I moved on to 7th grade, my next teacher, Miss Lowe, said, "Lola, I hear you like to draw." She stretched out a roll of brown wrapping paper and mounted a long piece on one long wall of the classroom. I drew characters and scenes from some of my favorite stories, and my classmates colored in my drawings. My favorite was my drawing of Ichabod Crane from "The Legend of Sleepy Hollow." I drew scenes from stories for two years.

A Special Christmas

As children, my brothers and sisters and I didn't have many toys. My sisters and I always yearned for dolls that were really special. I wanted a doll that had long hair and a dress and pretty lace underwear and shoes. A doll that could cry. One day, when I was in the 4th grade, Barbara and I went downtown to the Thompson Hardware store in Round Lake, and we picked out two dolls. She wanted the baby doll, and I wanted the little girl doll. We told the lady at the store that those were the dolls we wanted, but we didn't think we'd get them.

That year was Julane's first year teaching, and when she came home to Round Lake one weekend before Christmas, she went out and bought gifts for everyone in the family and hid them in the house. That next week, after she'd gone back to teaching, Barbara and I went upstairs to Julane's room and snooped around. Under a blanket, there were those two dolls that we had picked out at the hardware store! Julane had bought them for us! I suppose while Julane was shopping for gifts for our family, the lady who ran the store told her that Barbara and Lola wanted those dolls. How else would she have known? Regardless of how she knew, Julane bought them for us and hid them under a blanket.

After discovering those dolls, Barbara and I every day would go sneak a peek at them. One Saturday when Julane was back home, visiting, she caught us looking at those dolls. Uh-oh! We knew we were in trouble. She got after us. She said, "You're not going to get those dolls! You've been looking at them every day, and just because of that you're not going to get those dolls." We thought that was fair; after all, we weren't supposed to be snooping around in her room. On Christmas, though, Julane gave us the dolls after all. They were beautiful. They had stuffed bodies, but their legs and arms were made of glass. They had gorgeous clothes, darling underwear, and shoes. Barbara's baby doll made a sound like she was crying "Mama" when you patted her on the back. Mine had real hair. Barbara kept hers all her life. That was an extra special Christmas that year.

Church in Worthington

IN ROUND LAKE, THERE WEREN'T many big families like ours. There were only three families in that whole town that had as many children as we had in ours, while back in Granada there had been quite a few. Maybe that's why it took us all a little while to settle in and make new friends, but we eventually did.

Although there were churches in Round Lake, my parents joined the Methodist church in Worthington, Minnesota, which was 11 miles to the northwest, because they knew the pastor there, Pastor Groenig. He had been a pastor of theirs in Granada, and after we moved, he came out to visit us and asked my folks to join the Methodist church where he was serving in Worthington. It was a long distance from our new farm in Round Lake, especially since we were used to traveling half a mile to our church in Granada, but they joined and were members there all the rest of their lives. We didn't really attend the Sunday School at the church in Worthington as much as we probably could have. Sometimes Barbara and I would skip, because we didn't know the kids.

However, because Worthington was so far away, and because it was difficult to get there, especially in winter on those bad roads, we also ended up sometimes attending the Presbyterian church in Round Lake. Mother joined that church's women's group, and we attended Sunday School and Vacation Bible School there. I made a lot of friends in Vacation Bible School. The church in Round Lake had a lot of activities for the youth when I was growing up. The pastor there, John Mulholland, was very up and coming—kind of ahead of his time. He was open to having a variety of activities suitable for all different kinds of people. For instance, the church would have Halloween parties where we would bob for apples. There were also parties at Christmastime and on Valentine's Day. The people who attended those parties weren't all Presbyterians; anybody could go. I still have the letter Pastor John wrote to me when I graduated from high school. There was another church in Round Lake, too. It was a Lutheran church. They had a lot of activities going on, too, and we occasionally went there as well.

Girls Scouts and 4-H

I ALWAYS WENT STRAIGHT HOME every day after school on the bus. I wasn't friends with many of the town kids, but I was involved in other activities, such as Girl Scouts and 4-H. We joined the 4-H club when we were quite young. I didn't raise animals for 4-H, although my sisters and brothers did. I did cooking and baking. When I was 10 years old, I won a blue ribbon at the county fair for a white cake I baked. My mother taught me to bake bread when I was only 10, and I excelled in baking. I also won a lot of prizes for my various demonstrations. My food demonstrations earned me three trips to the Minnesota State Fair. I won lots of cooking utensils as prizes, and I once won a state award. That's where my speaking skills came in, because you had to talk to do a demonstration. That's where I showed confidence. Even though I was still shy and didn't feel adequate in social situations, when it came to public speaking, I came out of my shell. Even later, during my high school years, I won many awards in speech contests.

Memories of My Siblings

By the time I was born, Jerald, my oldest brother, was almost 11 years old. Nevertheless, I remember him very well. My relationship with my brother Jerald has been super throughout my entire life. He was an extraordinary, kind, wonderful human being. As a boy, he was hardworking and obedient. The year he graduated from high school was when Dad bought the land at Round Lake. The family couldn't move until March, so my brother Jerald went and lived all alone in that house for all of that time. He was such a help to my dad.

Julane was nine years old when I was born. We all looked up to Julane. She was the leader, and she always maintained that leadership role. She had a presence in a room. She was very articulate, and when she talked, you listened. She always had that gift. She had many friends. She was a bright, gifted child. Julane could read when she was only four. When she entered 1st grade, Jerald was in the 3rd grade. But the country school moved Jerald back a grade, and Julane was moved up a grade. She was a salutatorian of her high school graduating class. She played the piano for the church when she was 12. She took care of me a lot when I was growing up, and she did a lot of the cooking and cleaning and was a big help to Mother. When I was in high school, I used to wear her discarded teaching clothes.

Julane was about 20 and teaching near Worthington, when she married a local farmer. She wasn't supposed to be married while she was working as a teacher in the country school, so she and her husband tried to keep it a secret. She left on a Friday night in February and married him in Iowa. But the news of their marriage ended up in the local newspaper, so her employers found out. She was such an excellent teacher that they overlooked it and allowed her to stay.

After Julane, my next oldest sibling was my brother Woody. He turned eight soon after I was born. I had a good relationship with Woody. I got along especially well with all my brothers, mainly because I was an outdoor kid and they were outside with me. Not only did I spend a lot of my time outdoors doing chores to help my mother, but I also spent a lot of time in the grove climbing trees. While I was outside, my sisters were inside, so you can see the relationship with my brothers would naturally be stronger. It was through Woody that I later went to the Lutheran Bible Institute in Minneapolis.

My sister Carmen was six years older than I, and we were different from each other in some ways. For instance, she enjoyed housework and decorating. But what we had in common was that we both liked to read a lot. She was a leader in 4-H, and after she got her driver's license, she drove us to different 4-H activities. She was always active in church. By the time I got to high school, she was working as a teacher. I would get her castoff clothes, the ones that she didn't want anymore. I thought I was really well dressed, you know, with those fancy teaching clothes. When she got married and moved up near Cambria, Minnesota, I would sometimes go up and stay with her. She had certain stores where she liked to shop. We went shopping together, and she helped me pick out clothes.

Next in line was my brother Gordy. He was almost four when I was born. Gordy was always just a lot of fun! He laughed a lot and had an easygoing demeanor. He'd always say, "How is my beautiful sister?" or "How's my good-looking sister today?" Things like that. He was a loving, loveable man. During the war years, while I was in high school, I used to like washing my hair in melted snow water because I thought it made my hair look nicer than using our hard well water. I washed my hair only once a week in those days. Every Sunday, I'd collect snow in a great big container. I would melt all that snow water and put it in the big tub. Well, at that time, Gordy was dating the student nurses in Worthington, and he wanted nice hair, too. I had to learn to share my snow water with him before his weekend dates. Mother would encourage me to share, rather than taking it all for myself, so that's what I would do.

Stan was my buddy all of his life. He was just two years older, and our temperaments also matched: we were both shy, and we both eventually grew out of it. Best of all, we were both book people and loved reading. Stan and I together climbed many trees and rolled big tires around my dad's 640-acre farm.

My sister Barbara was born when I was three. She was our family's baby girl. Barbara and I often played together when we were young. Barbara was always meticulous and neat. During grade school, we had a small playhouse out in the grove on our farm. We got it all cleaned up—she was good at that—and played house. When workers at the farm would eat in that little playhouse and mess it up, that used to really bother Barbara. She was an excellent student and graduated with high honors. She also had the gift of sociability.

My youngest sibling, Doug, was born when I was seven. He was also an excellent student. In junior high, one of his teachers said that when he didn't know an answer, he'd ask Doug. He was not a social kid, but he was brilliant. He later became a pastor and a school principal. He was not outgoing like Gordy or Woody; he was a quiet man, but people who knew him respected him.

A Close Call with Stan

During one especially dry year, the summer before I was in 5th grade, my dad had Stan and me take the cattle over to the southern part of our farm to graze. We led them one mile east and one mile south to where there was good grass. Stan rode the pony on the south part, and I walked on the north part. We sent the cattle back and forth across that one piece of land. Of course I took along a stack of magazines and read about J. Edgar Hoover and the FBI while the cattle were grazing. (Remember this was in the 1930s.)

My dad was quite strict about the amount of time we grazed them. Dad never wanted us home too early and insisted that we stay out with them most of the day. Well, one day, at noon, the weather looked dark and threatening and a little wind started picking up. Stan and I talked it over. Stan said, "I think we better go home, but what will Dad say?" We decided to get going earlier than usual. And what happened next was an experience I will never forget. Had we not acted fast, I wouldn't be here today to tell it.

To lead the cattle back to the grove on my folks' place, we had to go north about a mile, and then head west another mile. While we were on our way home, the sky suddenly started to darken. It was almost black. We knew a big storm was coming in and coming in quick. Stan said, "Lola, you better get over to the fence." We both moved to the fence, east of the cattle, and just like that, in one minute, the rain came down in torrents! And hailstones came straight down, hard! The cattle turned and stampeded east. If we had waited one minute more, we would have been killed. I can still see it. I can smell the dust kicked up by the stampede. The cattle were racing toward the hired man's house. Stan and I walked back to the hired man's house, which was about three-quarters of a mile from my folks' place, and they telephoned my dad and said that we were safe. Dad came and got us in a wagon. I bet he was pretty shaken up because he never had us go out with the cattle again.

My Responsibilities

BY THE TIME WE GOT to Round Lake, I was old enough to help my mother in the kitchen more, mostly by baking bread and cookies.

I also helped her in our yard around our house in Round Lake, which was all mud when we moved in that March. Right away, Mother planted grass and flowers, and soon it was very lovely around there.

In the spring, I helped with the chickens; Mother had a lot of them. And I helped in the barn by cleaning the separator for the milk, which we used to separate the cream from the rich whole milk.

Accident on Our Swing

IN THE GROVE ON OUR farm in Round Lake, my brother Stan and I put up tree swings. We tied a long rope to the top of the tree and attached it to a sturdy stick on the bottom. We'd put our legs around the stick and swing back and forth. One afternoon during the summer before I entered 7th grade, when everyone else in our family had gone to Worthington and I was all alone, I went out to swing in the grove. I swung way out, and the rope suddenly snapped right at the very top of the branch. I took a bad fall and was in a lot of pain. I think I passed out but somehow made it back to the house. I remember lying on the bed with the whole family standing around, looking at me and wondering what to do.

Mom and Dad decided to take me that night to the hospital in Ocheyedan, Iowa, about 12 miles south of Round Lake. The next morning, the doctor in Ocheyedan, Dr. Pageant, tried to relocate my shoulder and set the broken bones in my arm, but he realized my injuries were so severe that he could not take care of me. He put me in a cast that looked like a vest—it covered me totally from waist to shoulders—and arranged for my parents to take me immediately to the University Hospital in Minneapolis. I was in the hospital for six weeks.

First, doctors had to get my arm straightened out and my shoulder back in the correct position. They drilled holes in my elbow and inserted pins into the holes. From the pins they hung weights to pull my shoulder down and keep it in the proper position while it healed. I had to lie flat on my back in the hospital bed with my arm suspended straight out for three weeks! At 13 years old!

After my shoulder and arm healed, I was able to get back up, but I still wasn't able to use my arm. It just hung down by my side; I couldn't move it at all. Next, they sent me down to the first floor of the hospital for intensive therapy. They tried a lot of new therapies on me. They used a lot of heat on my arm and had me do exercises in which I had to lift my arm up and down. Physical therapy was a new science back then.

Every day I would take the elevator on my own from the third floor to the first floor for therapy. And within three weeks, I was able to use my arm again.

The hospital was right by the Mississippi River, and every day after therapy I'd sneak outside and sit on the riverbank and watch the activity on the river. It just fascinated me. I felt like Tom Sawyer! I fell in love with the Mississippi River. Then I would go back in and take the elevator up to my room on the third floor. I never told anybody about sneaking outside, and no one ever found out.

While I was in the hospital in Minneapolis, I suddenly became aware of the excitement of the "big city." I met such a variety of people in the hospital—lots of other children and of course the doctors and nurses. The experience whetted my appetite for more adventures.

A Second Movie

THE YEAR AFTER MY ACCIDENT on the swing, I had a more pleasant memorable experience when I got to see my second movie. By then I was in 7th grade. On a beautiful Sunday, my parents' friends, Belle and John Sather, invited Mom, Dad, Barbara, and me to a lovely dinner at their home in Worthington. They served it just like in the magazines that I read—with china, silver, and table linens. It was beautiful to see and delicious to taste. Then they invited us to the theater to see a movie—*The Wizard of Oz*. After that, I told Mom I wanted to look like Judy Garland, so she braided my long blond hair every day.

My Deepening Love of Reading

As I grew older, I became more and more interested in reading good literature. I always had a stack of books under my bed. I learned to love classic literature. I read books like *Anne of Green Gables* and *Little Women*. I liked *Little Women* because I could relate the four girls in the March family to the four girls in my family. My sisters and I would all debate which one we most identified with. Which one of us was Meg? Which one was Jo? Which one was Beth, and which one Amy? I thought I was most like either Beth or Amy. The oldest girl, Meg, was very sweet; I didn't think I was like her. And I wasn't as nice as Beth. I loved art like Amy did. I used to draw all the time. But I also identified with Jo because Jo was free-spirited, like me. I was a spunky child. As the seventh in our family, I had learned to control that spunkiness.

In high school, my reading choices expanded further when my 9th-grade English teacher introduced me to Charlotte Brontë's *Jane Eyre*. I also read a lot of Shakespeare. I took Latin, and I loved history. In fact, I still do!

My mother and I would often visit the Carnegie Library in Worthington, where we would both check out books. I would visit with the librarian, Mrs. Humiston, and would read in front of the fireplace. Mother liked to read romances, but she would also read classics. She read a whole series about a family that came from England and settled in Canada. We used to read all the Robert Louis Stevenson books. We also read Rudyard Kipling and lots of Washington Irving.

Relationships with Mother and Father

I think each one of us children was special to Mother. With so many children and with so much work to get done, she had to be organized to divide her time among us. Of course, my parents didn't have a lot of activities outside the home, so they could concentrate on us. During my high school years, Mother spent quite a bit of time with me because the older girls were all gone from home by then. In high school, I had a close relationship with both my parents.

My dad was a very pleasant man. He loved cars! He had an affinity for big cars and always drove Buicks and Mercurys. During my high school years, Dad played the violin in the community orchestra in Worthington. He was very proud of that because here he was a farmer, and he was playing with men who had college educations.

I remember when I was a teenager, my father was very watchful over us. He had a good reputation, and he was concerned about us being decent, good people with equally good reputations. When I was in high school, he took us to all the basketball games. He always stayed there for the whole game and then drove us home. He was watchful about boys and gave me some good advice before I started dating. I've always appreciated that.

War Years

World War II started during my high school years, and I was very aware of what was going on. The day Pearl Harbor was attacked was an awful day. I remember our shock when we heard the news over the radio. I will never forget the expressions on my mother's and dad's faces. It was a dark time. Those are days you don't want to remember because of the mental darkness of it—like a dark cloud hanging over us. It was sad and hard. We listened to the radio for updates because we didn't have TV. We feared what might happen if the Allies didn't win.

The war was especially hard on my mother because three of her boys were in the service. My brothers Jerald and Woody were medics in the Army. Jerald served in the Pacific way over by Japan, and Woody was right in the middle of it all in London. Jerald drove an ambulance, and Woody retrieved people from the battlefields in mainland Europe. There were pictures of him looking real depressed, taking injured people off the ambulance. Stan was a paratrooper, but he didn't enter the military until the end of the war, so he missed the fighting. The military allowed Gordy to stay behind to help my dad on the farm.

Mother wrote to her sons every week while they were in the service. In high school we used to write to our different classmates who were in the military. The war affected our day-to-day lives in many ways. Gas was rationed, so you couldn't go anywhere. You couldn't make anything with sugar because it was also rationed. I remember when President Roosevelt died. And when the war was finally over, how happy we all were—it was just a wonderful, light feeling.

When my brothers came home from the service, they got on with their lives. Jerald married Lenore Sampson, a teacher, and they lived on the acreage west of our home in the house that had been the hired man's quarters. Jerald worked as a farmer. Woody went to the Lutheran Bible Institute in Minneapolis, where he met a nurse, whom he married. He became a Lutheran pastor. Gordy stayed on our family's farm. Stan married and then went to university and became a veterinarian.

Graduating from High School

UNLIKE MOST OF THE GIRLS I knew, I didn't have an interest in boys when I was in high school. Isn't that strange? I used to interview people for my high school newspaper, and I'd ask girls in my school, "What is your goal?" Their answer was always, "To get married young and have a family." That was *their* goal, but it was not *my* goal. My goal was to go to college. Marriage was on my mind, too, but I always wanted to get my college education first, then get married and have a family.

This was during wartime, and a lot of girls I knew had boyfriends in the military. They got married young and didn't go to college. I thought that might happen to me: I might fall for somebody in high school and never get to college, and that's not what I wanted. That's why I didn't really date a lot while I was in high school. I figured the time for marriage and a family would come; it would all fall into place. And it did.

When I graduated from high school in 1944, I received the American Legion Award for "Good Citizenship." My high school English teacher wanted me to go to St. Olaf College, an excellent private liberal arts college in central Minnesota. When I was a senior, he said, "You should go there." If I'd had my choice, that's where I would have gone, and I would have majored in English. But I couldn't afford to go to a private college.

Lola's high school graduation picture, Round Lake, 1944.

Chapter Four

Becoming a Teacher

Although my dad had not gone to school beyond 8th grade, both he and my mother encouraged all of us to pursue higher education. But with such a large family, they couldn't afford to send us to college. We had to pay for our own education. Any money our parents spent on us, we paid them back.

When Julane graduated from high school, she was sent to what was called a "teacher training program" in Fairmont. The teacher training programs offered a year of training, and then you went out and taught in a country school. Julane saved the money she earned teaching, so she could go to college in the summer. That's the only way she could get a college education. So following her lead, that's what I did, too. My goal wasn't to be a teacher. My goal was to get to college. But you had to get money in order to go to college, and teaching was one way to get the money. In my time, there weren't many professional options for girls. You could be a nurse, a teacher, or a secretary. Those were about your only options.

When I graduated from high school, my parents found a teacher training program for me in the town of Blue Earth, and I went there for a year. My mentor teacher was Marian Drake, whose wardrobe consisted of five dresses, one for every day of the week. We trainees received hands-on training to teach grades 1st to 8th in a rural school. Blue Earth was a pretty town on a river; I especially remember the poignant aroma of burning leaves in the fall. While I was finishing up, schools were being consolidated and teaching opportunities were tightening up, but I fortunately still landed a teaching job.

Teaching in Country Schools

I SPENT MY FIRST YEAR as a teacher in a country school near Rushmore, Minnesota, west of Worthington. I taught there from fall of 1945 through spring of 1946. A lot of the older women who taught in the country schools for years and years had their own cars, so they could live in town and drive to work. Since I didn't have a car, I lived in the country with the Herman Wick family and walked to school each day. The Wicks were an older couple that had a son who was still single living with them. They were very good people, and they were good to me. Mrs. Wick prepared very good food, which I carried to school in a pail for lunch. It was inconvenient to wash my hair and clothes at the Wicks' home, so on Friday nights I'd stay at the school to wash my hair and to do my laundry. I'd hang my clothes on a line in the school, and when I'd get back to the school on Monday morning, I'd take them down.

When the weather got cold in the fall, I had to start the school's furnace going, but I was 19 years old and knew nothing about furnaces. The furnace produced a lot of smoke, but I could not get that thing going! Finally, in October, I told the school board about the trouble I was having with the furnace. Their first answer was, "The other teachers never complained." I finally got Mr. Wick to come to the school and get it going for me. All he had to do was tighten up the grates so the coal wouldn't fall through. And then it worked. That's all it was. It wasn't that big of a deal, but I didn't know, being so young.

Lola, 1952.

In that country school in Rushmore, I had 20 students in 1st through 8th grades. I had two 8th graders, and at the end of the school year, they were going to have to take state boards. If they didn't pass them, that would be a serious offense against the teacher, so I was really worried about that. All year I worked really hard with those 8th graders so they would do well. They did pass, and that helped me feel more confident.

I was really tickled by how much progress my four 1st graders made; they learned how to read really well that year. I loved listening to those four 1st graders read! I had never taught anybody to read before, and I was just delighted with them. I loved that part of the job.

At the end of that school year, three men knocked on my door. They introduced themselves as members of the board of a different school district. They said they'd heard from the school superintendent about what a beautiful job I'd done teaching reading to my 1st graders, and they were offering me a position in a different school, up by Reading, about 22 miles northwest of Round Lake. The position they were offering was to teach 1st through 4th grades. That sounded like a better job to me, so I accepted their offer. That summer, I enrolled in classes at Mankato State College, about 100 miles northeast of Round Lake. I was able to pay for my tuition because I'd saved most of the money I'd earned as a teacher.

In the fall of 1946, I started my second year of teaching in the country school near Reading. I lived with friends of my parents, Harry and Jenny Clark. That was a wonderful year. The Clarks treated me like a daughter, and I was teaching in a nicer, better-equipped school. Although this school also didn't have indoor plumbing or electricity, it had a better coal-burning stove, and I had only four grades to teach and only about 10 students. About the only excitement I had that year was when a weasel was standing in the door of the coal shed and wouldn't let me in.

Overall, I had a very, very nice situation, but at the end of that year, the school board closed the school because enrollment was too low. They were consolidating schools, so I was out of a job.

At that point, I decided I didn't want to teach in any more country schools. The jobs were drying up as country schools were phased out, but there were other reasons besides that. In the country schools, I had to do all the janitorial work: I had to clean, sweep the floor, haul in the coal. All that. Plus I was lonely out in the country. Even though I'm somewhat shy, I'm also a people person, and I like to have people around me. Since I'm from a big family, I'm used to having lots of people around. Out in the country, I spent a lot of time by myself, with no adults to talk to. I decided I'd have to find another type of job. Although I had saved most of the money I'd earned during my second year of teaching, that summer I worked at a camp instead of taking college courses. Going to college was still my goal, but by then I'd met Bob Geisendorfer, and that changed my life forever.

The Wilson family, 1946. Top row, from left: Arthur Gordon and Stanford Joel. Middle row, from left: Woodrow Warren, Lola Mae, Carmen Lillian, Thora Julane, and Jerald Oliver. Bottom row, from left: Barbara Ann, Jacob Oliver, Anna Geneva, and Douglas Alan.

Chapter Five

Meeting Bob

While I was teaching in the country school near Reading, I often would go home to Round Lake on the weekends. On those visits, my sister Barbara and I sometimes went to a bowling alley in Worthington while my folks were at the store in town getting groceries. Of course what do girls do? We talked to the boys! By then, I was 20 and had gotten over the idea that I wasn't going to date.

One of the boys we met one night at that bowling alley was Bob Geisendorfer, my future husband. When Bob introduced himself to us, I recognized his name right away. We were about the same age (Bob was a little younger, by six months), but we hadn't gone to high school together because he was from Worthington. He didn't know me. But I'd heard all about him. I knew the Worthington boys because the Round Lake town girls would talk about them. And even though I didn't date in high school, I was interested in what the other girls had to say about the Worthington boys, including Bob. Also, I knew just from reading the local newspaper that Bob's father was chief of police in Worthington and that his family went to First Lutheran Church.

When we met, in the spring of 1947, Bob had just gotten out of the Navy, and he was attending Worthington Junior College. He had joined the Navy right after graduating from high school, and he was stationed at the naval base in Chicago. I don't think he served for very long because he graduated from high school in 1945, and when we met in 1947, he already was in junior college studying business.

Bob's high school photo, Worthington, Minnesota, 1945.

The same night I met Bob, Barbara met another boy, and they asked to take us home to Round Lake. That was a Saturday night. On the way home, Bob asked me out on a date to the movies for the following night, and I accepted.

I suppose Bob decided that he wanted to find out more about me before our date, so the day after we met at the bowling alley, he and his friend went around Round Lake asking people about Barbara and me. Bob wanted to go with a girl who had a good reputation, so he went to all the bars in town to find out if the Wilson girls would pass the reputation test. Remember my dad told us about having a good reputation? People at the bars told Bob and his friend that my sister and I were very good girls, so we passed the test. (Since I knew of his family and already knew they had a good name, I didn't have to check on him.)

Bob during his service in the Navy, Chicago, circa 1945–47.

The next evening, Bob came to my house to take me to the movies. I don't remember what we saw. He drove all the way to Round Lake to pick me up in his folks' car. (He lived with his parents then.) That was pretty much the first real date I'd been on. The year before, when I was teaching in the country school, I'd had a gentleman friend, but it wasn't anything serious. After that first date, I dated Bob continually. I was teaching near Reading during the week, but we would see each other on weekends. We often would go to a movie on Sunday nights. That's the way it was, only once a week. At the end of that school year, I went with him to his college prom.

When I first met Bob, and when I went on that first date with him, I remember feeling comfortable with him. That's a hard thing to explain; I was just comfortable with him right away. He was quite serious but nice. Right off the bat, I noticed he had the qualities that I liked in a man: easy to talk to, kind, soft-spoken, and respectful. But at that time, I didn't feel like committing myself until I had my own life straightened out.

Moving to Minneapolis

THE SUMMER OF 1947, FOLLOWING my year teaching in the country school near Reading, I took a job working for six weeks at a church camp on beautiful Lake Pepin, which borders Wisconsin and Minnesota, on the Mississippi River. I loved lying on the beach and watching the activity on the lake at night. Since I was away at camp all summer, I only saw Bob once, when he came to visit me.

I saved most of the money I earned working at the camp and was hoping to be able to enroll in college at Mankato State in the fall. But as fall approached, I realized I wasn't going to have enough money saved, and I just didn't know what I was going to do. My brother Woody suggested that I attend the Lutheran Bible Institute (LBI) in Minneapolis. He had graduated from there, and it was not very expensive to attend. I could work part-time and go to school part-time. I liked the idea of living in Minneapolis. It was a wonderful city to live in, particularly for single people in their 20s. It's a beautiful place with lots of art, plays, and activities. So I took my brother's advice and enrolled at LBI.

I found a job working for the Harold Holden family on Minnehaha Parkway in Minneapolis. The family consisted of Mr. Holden, his wife, Harriet, and their three children: Hal, 4th grade; Judy, 1st grade; and Georgie, age 2. The Holdens treated me like one of the family. My responsibilities included taking care of the children, helping with the housework, and doing all the cooking for the family. I made the meals every single night. I baked a lot of cookies, and every Saturday I'd bake a fancy cake. I was well prepared to handle the food since I'd been learning how to cook and bake since I was 10 years old.

In the mornings, I would head to LBI, where I took classes in Bible studies and on teaching methods. A lot of the people taking classes at LBI went on to serve as missionaries and also as parish or youth workers in the church.

In the afternoons, I would return to the Holdens' home to take care of little Georgie. Mrs. Holden was gone quite a bit because she was involved in lots of activities in Minneapolis. When the older children came home from school each day, I was there to greet them.

On Saturdays, I stayed at the house and worked all day. On Sunday mornings, I went to church along with the Holden family at the Hennepin Avenue Methodist Church. At noon, I would always prepare a big chicken dinner and do all the dishes. Then I would go off for the evening. I befriended some of the other young people at church and at school, and we would go out to all the church activities on Sunday nights. Occasionally, I attended plays in the city. It was a wonderful experience for a country girl. For any girl, for that matter! I loved Minneapolis, and I wanted to stay there.

That whole year I saw Bob only twice. He was back in Worthington, going to community college. He came up to see me in Minneapolis once, and I came home once. I had just started going with him the previous spring, and I liked him, but I was in Minneapolis and we were not going steady yet. I met a few other guys while I was living in Minneapolis, but nothing serious developed with any of them. There was a fellow from Carleton College who was interested in me; he would come up and see me. There was another nice young man, a fellow student at the Bible Institute, whom I met later on in the fall of 1947. I don't even remember his name. Starting around Christmastime that year, he and I would sit together in the library every day in between classes when we had a break. We would study the Bible together and attend activities on Sunday nights, but it was just a friendship; that was all. At the end of the 1947–48 school year, he and I went to a graduation ceremony for the students of the Bible Institute, and this young man asked me, "Lola, are you going to come back in the fall?" I said, "I don't know." And I'll never forget this: He said, "I hope so." I was still free to date whomever I wanted at that point because I was not going steady with anybody. My goal was still to go to college before I moved ahead toward marriage.

At the end of that school year, Mrs. Holden asked me, "Now what are you going to do, Lola?" I said, "I don't know. I don't have any money to go to college, and I don't know what I'm going to do." I told her I was planning to teach for six weeks in the summer at Bible school, which would give me some money, but not enough to attend college full-time. Mrs. Holden said to me: "You're a lovely girl, Lola. I belong to a group that gives scholarships to girls for college, and I'll put your name down. I know you won't have any problems getting a scholarship if the recommendation comes from me." So that's what happened. I applied for that scholarship, and I had no problem getting it. Just think: my goal was to go to college, and now I had a scholarship!

During the summer of 1948, I taught for six weeks at a Bible school in Coon Valley, Wisconsin. I earned enough money to spend the rest of the summer in classes at Mankato State.

With the scholarship I'd received, I could have afforded to continue at Mankato State in the fall, but at that point I wasn't too fond of that school, and I wasn't excited about going there. I really wanted to go to college at St. Olaf, but my scholarship wouldn't cover the costs of enrolling in a private college. I thought about going back up to the Lutheran Bible Institute. After all, Harriet Holden wanted me back working for her, and I loved Minneapolis so much. But by then I was getting more serious with Bob, and Minneapolis was a long way from Worthington. I knew I wanted to go to college somewhere, but I just didn't know what to do. I was in a quandary.

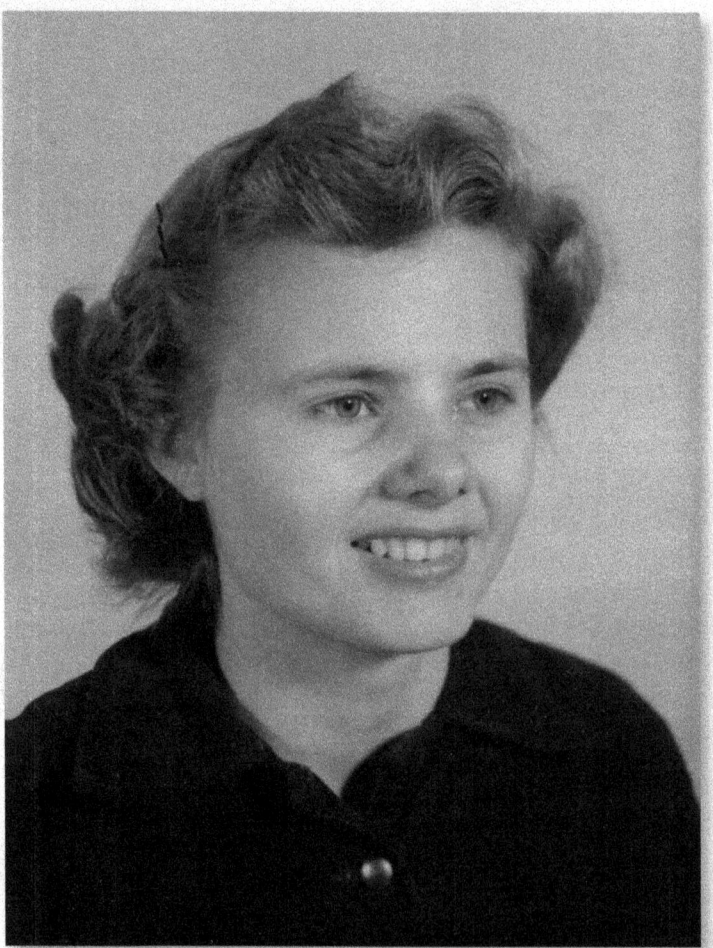

Lola, Ocheyedan, Iowa, 1948.

Teaching in Ocheyedan, Iowa

At this point, my dad was on the school board at Round Lake. In August, a week before school started, he heard about an opening for a 5th-grade teacher in the little town of Ocheyedan. If I were to teach in Ocheyedan, I would be able to live very close to home and close to Bob.

While my goal was still to go to college, I also had a goal to teach in town, and this was a good town school. Even though I hadn't yet earned my two-year degree, I had enough college credits to qualify for the teaching position in Ocheyedan. Hiring policies weren't as strict then as they are now.

Dad heard about the job opening on a Monday night. The next day, I went down to Ocheyedan, met the superintendent, and got the job. I felt great about that. I'd be teaching 5th grade! Just one grade! Teaching just one grade sure was going to be easier than teaching 1st through 8th, as I had in the first country school where I taught. Since I didn't have enough money to attend the college I wanted, I decided I would take the teaching job and save my money to attend Mankato State in the summers.

In Ocheyedan, I rented a room in the home of a couple named the Heislers, who lived right across the street from the school. Usually, I ate my dinner downtown at a restaurant.

I just loved my job in Ocheyedan. It was a wonderful school with lovely kids. I didn't have to do any janitorial work, and there was no furnace to worry about! And at this school, I had colleagues. We had a very wonderful faculty. I still hear from some of the teachers I taught with back then. We even had somebody to teach music. Oh, it was just heaven!

Another big plus was that Ocheyedan is just 17 miles north of Worthington, so after I moved there, Bob and I were able to start seeing each other more often, and our relationship deepened. From the way I saw it, that's when we started going steady. I don't know how he felt, though. Maybe he always thought of me as his girl, but I felt that since we hadn't had an agreement between us before then, I was open to meet others.

During that year, Bob and I would see each other just on weekends, usually on Sunday nights. We'd often go to the movies or we might visit my folks in Round Lake, and we'd ride about—that type of thing.

Ready for Marriage

At the end of the 1948–49 school year, I went back to Mankato State for the summer session. As I said, Mankato State was not my top choice, but I had to make a decision, and it was good enough.

Meanwhile, Bob was spending the summer back in Worthington, 96 miles southwest of Mankato, working at the Minnesota Natural Gas Company. Near the start of the first summer session, he came up to visit me, and while we were sitting in his car, he just all of a sudden proposed.

Marrying Bob was absolutely the thing I wanted to do. He was everything that I wanted in a husband—he was good, honest, kind, and from a good, stable family. We were comfortable together, and we got along well together. He was very kind to my family. He was what I would call a good, stable man. He was always, always that way. I was not wrong in choosing Bob. It was the right thing to do. I feel fortunate that we found each other. I wanted to get married and have a family, but I also still was determined to get a college education. So I accepted Bob's proposal, but I said to him, "I'm not going to get married until I get that two-year degree. I'm going to go to college all summer long, and I'm not going to get married until I'm done." You see, you could teach with a two-year certificate in those days. I refused to get married without it because I knew that I would have a hard time getting a teaching job without that certificate. I had seen people who didn't have their degree, and they didn't get the positions they tried for in the schools. I thought it was a wise thing to do. And by that point, I was close to completing my two-year degree. All I had to do was finish two more summers of college. By the end of the summer of 1950, I would have enough credits to earn my two-year certificate. Of course, I had always wanted a four-year degree, but marrying Bob had become more important to me by then.

Balancing Goals and Dreams

Bob agreed to wait, and he was always pleased afterward that I'd made that decision. Finishing up my two-year degree at Mankato State opened up opportunities for me that I otherwise wouldn't have had.

We weren't officially engaged until Valentine's Day of 1950. That's when he gave me a ring and we announced our engagement to our families and to the public and started planning our wedding.

Later, the advisor at Mankato State during my practice teaching had asked me, "Lola, what are you going to do now? You're college material, and you should continue and get your four-year degree." I told her, "But I'm getting married." She said, "I think that's the best choice, Lola. I've never been married, and if I would have had the choice, I would have done what you are doing."

In those days it was the best choice. That's what most women did. I made the decision to marry Bob by myself. When you're from a big family, the minute you graduate from high school, you're pretty much on your own. Any money that my siblings and I got from my parents, we'd pay it back. I lived with my parents on weekends and during some summers, but I supported myself. Even though it was my decision to marry Bob, my parents were very, very pleased with him. My mother said, "I never could tell you what to do, Lola, but I was always secretly hoping you would marry Bob." She said she realized that if she had said anything like, "I hope you marry him," I probably would have wanted to do the opposite. That's the way people are, when they're young.

Lola and Bob on their wedding day, August 20, 1950, Worthington, Minnesota.

Chapter Six

Married Life

Bob and I were married on August 20, 1950. Since I was planning to return to my teaching job in Ocheyedan in the fall of 1950, we purposely timed our wedding and honeymoon for the week before school started.

On my wedding day, I wore a ballerina-length organdy gown and a white, embossed organdy picture hat with a big brim. I wore long, white gloves in organdy sheer. We were married at the Methodist church in Worthington. We had a reception for our relatives right after the wedding. It was a small, simple, uncomplicated affair, nothing like the events people have nowadays. Right after the wedding and reception, Bob and I went off together on a wedding trip into Canada, to the North Shore of Lake Superior. Bob had his own car by then. It was a fun week. We both just fell in love with the North Shore drive, and I still love it.

When Mrs. Heisler, the woman I had been renting a room from in Ocheyedan, found out that I was getting married, she and her husband offered to make an apartment in the upstairs of their big house for Bob and me. They made it special, just for Bob and me, because they liked the two of us so much. It was very nice of them, and it worked out real well.

So Bob and I started our married life together in a nice little apartment. It had one bedroom and a kitchen with a stove. We even had our own private bathroom up there. We lived in that apartment for two years. It was right across the street from the school where I taught, and Bob drove to Worthington every day for work. By then he was working in the Worthington office of the Minnesota Natural Gas Company. He helped quite a bit with the drawing of maps. He'd taken some type of art class in college, so he could do the calligraphy work on those maps. He did beautiful work. He also installed gas furnaces and stoves, dug ditches, and worked in the office—he did all that. He was a very conscientious, capable man.

We lived in Ocheyedan for the next two years. During those first few years of marriage, before we had children, we both were working all week long, but we also had fun together. We'd see movies and sometimes eat out at restaurants. We made some very good friends with other married couples—friends that lasted a lifetime. One couple was Clinton and Sylvia Dahl. She was a teacher in the Ocheyedan system, and her husband taught nearby in the Harris, Iowa school system. Every Sunday night the four of us would get together. We'd have a meal and then play cards. They were our very dear friends.

After we got married, Bob and I went to church in Ocheyedan together. We continued at the same Methodist church that I'd been attending before our marriage. Bob and I also did some traveling together. We visited relatives and friends, and we went down to Okoboji, Iowa—a big resort town with places to eat, theaters, and one of the biggest freshwater lakes in the whole world.

Lola and Bob leaving church after getting married.

*Lola and Bob's wedding day, August 20, 1950, Worthington, Minnesota.
From left: Bob's brother, Jim; Bob; Lola; and Lola's sister Barbara.*

Wedding announcement for Lola and Bob that ran in the Worthington Daily Globe, Tuesday, August 22, 1950.

MR. AND MRS. ROBERT GEISENDORFER (Lola Mae Wilson) are shown leaving the First Methodist church after their marriage there Sunday afternoon. (Photo by Rickers)

* * *

Round Lake Girl, Local Man Wed in Methodist Church

The marriage of Lola Mae Wilson, daughter of Mr. and Mrs. J. O. Wilson, Round Lake, and Robert E. Geisendorfer, son of Mr. and Mrs. V. H. Geisendorfer, Worthington, was solemnized at the First Methodist church in Worthington, at 3 p. m. Sunday.

Dr. James Leach officiated at the double ring ceremony. The altar was decorated with garden flowers from the bride's home and candelabra. Mrs. Kenneth Jones, New Ulm, and Mrs. Byron Coyer, Worthington, sister of the bride, decorated the church.

Wedding marches from "Lohengrin" and by Mendelssohn were played by Kathleen Anderson. James Vance sang "The Lord's Prayer" and "Twenty third Psalm."

The bride was attired in a white embossed organdy over satin gown. It was ballerina length fashioned with a full skirt and fitted bodice and cap sleeves. A large satin bow was tied at the waist. She wore matching gauntlets, a picture hat and white linen pumps. Her jewelry was a gold bracelet and earrings of her mother's. She carried a colonial bouquet of talisman roses and white gladioli.

Barbara Wilson, sister of the bride, was maid of honor. She wore a gown similar in design to that of the bride's of lavender embossed organdy over taffeta. She carried a colonial bouquet of yellow roses and white carnations.

Best man was James Geisendorfer, brother of the bridegroom. Ushers were Gordon Wilson, brother of the bride, and Philip Anderson.

After the ceremony, a wedding luncheon was served to about 60 relatives and friends at the Gobbler cafe.

Douglas Wilson, brother of the bride, had charge of the guest book, and Mr. and Mrs. Woodrow Wilson, Minneapolis, had charge of the gifts.

The couple left for a week's trip to northern Minnesota and Duluth. They will be at home in Worthington where the bridegroom is employed by the Natural Gas company.

The bride is a graduate of Mankato State Teachers college and is teaching in Ocheyedan. The bridegroom is a graduate of Worthington Junior college.

Out-of-town guests were Mr. and Mrs. Wesley Navara, Lynn Marie and Bobby, Windom; Mr. and Mrs. Dean Kingery, Minneapolis; Mr. and Mrs. Elmer Nord, Iona; Mr. and Mrs. Henry Sampson, Windom; Mrs. Bert Prestholt and Karen, Lake Mills, Iowa; Mr. and Mrs. Harry Thompson and Mrs. Andrew Smith, Forest City, Iowa.

Mr. and Mrs. C. B. Larson, Brewster; Mr. and Mrs. J. O. Wilson, Douglas and Barbara, Mr. and Mrs. Jerald Wilson, Mary, Jeanne and Edith, Mr. and Mrs. Gordon Wilson and Stephan, Round Lake. Mr. and Mrs. Kenneth Jones, Kent and Katha, New Ulm; Mr. and Mrs. Woodrow Wilson, Minneapolis, and Mr. and Mrs. Worthis Usher, Estherville, Iowa.

The Geisendorfer Family

As soon as I started going with Bob, I got acquainted with his family. (I already knew who they were because we are a small community here.) I admired them. I knew I was marrying into a very fine family, and that was important to me. Bob's dad, Victor Henry Geisendorfer, was a very fine man. He was well respected as the chief of police in Worthington. He could trace his heritage back to 1620 in Germany. His grandfather, a pastor from Germany, started an orphanage down in Waverly, Iowa, for Civil War orphans.

Bob's mother, Anne Johnson Geisendorfer, was very much a family person. She was a wonderful mother and grandmother. She loved being a homemaker. Bob's mother had never worked outside the home, and she was living in the era when more and more women were starting to pursue careers.

Bob's sister, Marion, was about 10 years older than he. Marion and I had a very good relationship, and I was forever a friend of hers. Bob's brother, James, was about two years younger than he, and I also got along well with him. I still have close relationships with the Geisendorfer family. They are a very good, close-knit family.

Julie's Birth

After the end of the school year in 1952, Bob and I moved from Ocheyedan to Worthington and rented a cottage on the west side of the lake. We lived there for two years. I got a job teaching 5th grade in a public school in the little town of Reading, 10 minutes from our home in Worthington. To qualify for that position, I needed a two-year certificate, so it was good that I had earned it.

During the 1952–53 school year, I became pregnant with Julie. I was tired and nauseated at first, but then I started feeling better. I finished that school year but let the school know that I wouldn't be returning in the fall.

I was pregnant with Julie when Bob and I took a trip to California. We went to Los Angeles for the first time, which was exciting, and we visited Bob's aunt, who lived there. Then we headed up to San Francisco, and I fell in love with that city. The excitement of that beautiful city was the most thrilling thing for a girl from a farm!

Julie was born on November 19, 1953—a good, healthy baby. Of course, at that point, I wasn't even thinking about teaching anymore. Ever since I was a little girl, I always knew I wanted children. I thought becoming a mother was a very exciting experience. It was all new to me, and my mother came to Worthington and helped me.

When I first had Julie, I mostly focused on taking care of her, but I filled my time in other ways as well. I took knitting classes, did housework, and attended neighborhood coffee get-togethers. We had lots of lovely, sociable neighbors. Bob and I also became involved in church activities. When we moved back to Worthington, I joined his church, which was the First Lutheran Church, and I have been a Lutheran ever since.

Since Bob's folks lived in Worthington, they'd often have us over for meals. Bob's dad was having health problems by then, and he'd had to leave the police force, which was hard on him. He couldn't work anymore, and Bob's mom was taking care of him.

Lola and Julie, 1957.

Moving to Windom

IN THE SPRING OF 1954, Bob was offered the job of manager of the Minnesota Natural Gas Company in Windom, Minnesota, about 30 miles northeast of Worthington. The offer confirmed how capable and hardworking Bob was. I was happy to relocate to Windom because I thought it was a very good offer.

We rented a big house in Windom and moved into a nice neighborhood full of grandmothers; there were at least four older women living nearby who were all very kind neighbors.

Still, that was a stressful time. We left Worthington while Bob's dad was sick. We were living in a new town. Bob was adjusting to his new position as a manager, and because he was so conscientious, that caused extra stress. Plus, we had a toddler.

I also had to adjust to my life at home as a mother, but I had chosen it, so I liked it. I'm a people person, but I'm also a family person, and I was content to be home with Julie and very happy to be Bob's wife. He had a good profession, and I enjoyed being a wife and mother. I don't think I would have traded that for anything at all. I knew housework wasn't my strength, but I liked to cook, and I made homemade bread. In addition to caring for Julie, I occupied myself with other things: I watched a friend's children so she could go out; I attended a watercolors painting class; I did a lot of church and community work; and I always read a lot to myself and to Julie. When you're home alone with a child, having a hobby like reading is a good thing.

Since Bob's parents were retired, they were free to travel, visiting their children and grandchildren and other relatives. They would visit us in Windom once a week, and then once a week they would go to Luverne, Minnesota, where Marion lived. They did that because family was what was important to them.

Becky's Birth

WHILE WE WERE LIVING IN Windom, I became pregnant with our second child, Becky. I knew that I was pregnant because I was feeling tired, which I rarely do. I don't get tired. Even now in old age I have lots of energy. My pregnancy with Becky was completely easy. Even her delivery was easy. She was born on August 31, 1956. While I was in the hospital, Bob's parents, Anne and Vic, came up to stay with Julie, who was two and a half years old.

When Julie was born, the doctor had wanted me to breast-feed, but I wasn't able to do it. I don't know why, but I just didn't have any milk. By the time Becky was born, I was familiar with the bottle and comfortable preparing baby formula. The doctor recommended that since I couldn't breast-feed Julie, we should just go ahead with the bottle with Becky. I didn't fuss about it. The bottle was simple, so why not?

Julie was the kind of child who was content staying in the house. I took her outside for walks, but I spent a lot of time reading to her at home. Becky was different. As a little girl, she always wanted to be out in the neighborhood, getting acquainted with all the grandmothers. She would go from one grandmother's house to another, and they all enjoyed talking to Becky. She learned to talk early and was a sociable little girl.

Joel's Birth

I ALWAYS KNEW THAT I wanted three children, and that's what I got. Joel was born on June 19, 1960. By then, Julie was six going on seven, and Becky was three going on four. I was very happy that I could have three. Oh, my Joel was a happy baby! I had an easy pregnancy and delivery with him, too. His delivery took longer because he was a very big baby—he was eight pounds, bigger than the girls. I never had any problems with any of my pregnancies. And the doctor said they were the healthiest kids in town. I was always thankful for that.

Julie, age 5, and Becky, age 2, Windom, Minnesota, circa 1958.

"Finally, brethren, whatever is true, whatever is noble, whatever is right, whatever is pure, whatever is lovely, whatever is admirable—if anything is excellent or praiseworthy—think about such things. Whatever you have learned or received or heard from me—or seen in me—put it into practice. And the God of peace will be with you."
Philippians 4:8–9

Chapter Seven

Raising the Children

My husband was always supportive of the children, but he had a very stressful job that took up a lot of his time and energy. He had a two-year degree and then worked very hard to compete with men who had four-year degrees. His responsibilities were demanding: he was overseeing the building of pipelines and the delivery of natural gas supplies throughout the towns. He would get up every morning and leave for work by 8:00 a.m., and then he would get home at 5:00 p.m. He was always prompt that way, but he traveled quite a bit, too, especially later when he worked for Greeley Gas Company. He would fly to company headquarters in Greeley, Colorado, for a couple of days, and I'd be home alone with the kids.

Raising children was work. But I did it. We lived in a neighborhood where there were other children for them to play with, and the neighborhood grandmothers kind of watched over my kids, too. The kids remember lots of fun things they did. I didn't have a car to run around with, but I took the kids for lots of walks to the park. I did so much reading to them. I started taking them to the library when they were young, just as my mother had done with me. My son Joel tells me even nowadays just how much my reading to him meant to him.

Moving Back to Worthington

IN THE WINTER OF 1961, when Joel was one year old, Bob got a job offer to return to Worthington as manager of the Greeley Gas Company. He accepted the position and started his new job, but for several months, we continued living in our rental house in Windom, and Bob drove back and forth from Windom to Worthington each day.

In April of 1961, he found a house for us to purchase in Worthington. It was a nice house for a good price, close to a very good school, in a lovely neighborhood, and on the very end of the street.

The Geisendorfers' home at 1009 Elmwood Avenue, Worthington, 1961.

We purchased the house in about May but didn't move in till the summer. In July of 1961, we moved to 1009 Elmwood Avenue, the same house I live in today. It's still a great location: the golf course backs up to our yard, there's a park nearby to the south, and we can see the lake from our window.

I was happy to come back to Worthington. Bob had a company car that we both could use, but he used it to drive back and forth to work. I didn't need a car because everything in Worthington is within walking distance. The girls were in school by then, but Joel was just a toddler, and I'd take him for lots of walks to the parks. He also played with our pets, a Siamese cat called Figaro and later a dachshund called Heidi.

Our neighborhood was an ideal place for the children to grow up. There was a skating rink only a block away, a lake to swim in, and lots of places to run and play. The children also went ice-skating at a place called Whiskey Ditch, which was only a block away. They skated up and down that old dredge ditch.

After we moved back to Worthington, Grandma Anne and Grandpa Vic had us over every Sunday for dinner after church. She'd always have the same menu: a pot roast, a Jell-O salad, coleslaw, potatoes and gravy, and pie.

During the years when the three children were growing up, I was mainly focused on taking care of them and running the household. Keeping everything neat and in order didn't come naturally to me, so housework was challenging. I did like the food part, because I liked to cook. The children, Joel especially, remember the home-baked beans that I made a lot. My husband loved them, too. I cooked them in an original bean pot that I bought in Ocheyedan in 1951 for five cents at a dime store. (Joel still uses that bean pot to cook beans.)

Along with my family, I also was always involved in our church and our community. I taught Sunday School and Bible School. I was a Brownie leader for four years and a Cub Scout leader for Joel. I was real active in the Scouts, and I maintained a friendship with my associate leader. I met new people when we moved back to Worthington, and some of them are still my good friends to this day.

I really didn't have a lot of problems with the kids growing up because we lived in a good neighborhood. We allowed the children a lot of independence in that neighborhood. There were a lot of families with children when we moved in, and the kids all ran around together. Since we were so close to the lake, I insisted that my children all learn how to swim. They all took lessons at the Y, and later on my girls worked as lifeguards. (Years later, when Joel lost his kayak in Alaska, he was able to swim to safety in the huge ocean current. He was such a good swimmer that he survived.)

During summer vacations from school, my kids got quite a bit of playtime. They had good friends all the way through, and I believe that's important, too. Becky always loved horses, and she struck a deal with the owner of a horse: he told Becky that if she took care of the horse, she could ride him. She had a friend who also loved horses, and they rode together. Julie had a good friend who lived right on the lake in Worthington, and they had fun waterskiing together in the summer. All three children engaged in the various activities that went on in Worthington in the summer: swimming, tennis, going to parks, picnicking with the family, and running and biking around a lot.

The Teen Years

When I was in high school, my mother allowed me to be involved in many of the activities available in Round Lake. I thought that worked out well, so I decided that when my children reached their teens, they, too, should be involved in many activities. I thought that having experiences beyond their academic studies would help make them well-rounded and would be good for their growing-up years. All three of my children were confirmed at First Lutheran Church in Worthington, and they all sang in a church group called the Spiriters. Becky was in plays, the band, and practically every activity in high school you could be in. Julie taught Sunday School. Joel was into wrestling and performed in plays. He didn't finish growing until he was out of high school, so he was smaller than most of the other boys. He always said that some of the boys almost looked like men when they were in high school, but he looked like a little kid. In plays, he was given the part of Li'l Abner and other roles that called for a smaller person. When he graduated from high school, he was still only about 5'6". But he kept growing. It wasn't until later that Joel got to be the 6'2" guy that he is now. He didn't like being short in high school. But it wasn't a real problem for Joel because he was well liked.

Motivating the children to do well in school wasn't always easy. When you are a parent and your husband is gone a lot, you do your best to keep your children busy and on top of their schoolwork. You do your best by going to all the different parent-teacher conferences and by finding out how to work with the kids and with their teachers, too. Joel was an outdoor kid, and I think he was always thinking about what he could be doing outdoors. Even so, I always had good reports from all their teachers. They were good kids.

My worries during their teenage years came more from my concerns about what I thought *could* happen rather than what actually *did* happen. I felt very responsible for them all the time, so when they were running around town, I worried that they might get into trouble. I tried hard to be a good mother, but I probably didn't have as much expertise as I would have liked.

My children grew up differently from the way I was brought up. As an adolescent, I lived on the farm. Way out in the country, secluded; you can't run around every day with friends. You're just out there with your family.

The Geisendorfers, 1966. From left: Joel, Becky, Lola, Julie, and Bob.

The Geisendorfers, 1972. From left: Joel, Julie, Lola, Becky, and Bob.

My children grew up in town, closer to their friends, closer to everything. Maybe other mothers who had always lived in bigger towns and cities knew more about what to expect than I did. In my mind, parenting teenagers was very different from parenting young children. When they are teenagers, they are still with you, but not as much, because they're out and about. You don't feel you have the control that you have when they were younger.

Joe, Julie, and Becky. Worthington, 1976.

Reflections on Motherhood

I READ AN ARTICLE ONCE on choices. When you choose something and you know it's what you want, it works out well. From the very beginning, I planned my life. I chose to marry Bob. I chose to be a mother. It's what I wanted to be. I was comfortable in Worthington, and it was a very good place for the family to grow up. That's not to say that motherhood wasn't a challenge. It was, but I just accepted it that way. The way I dealt with things that were sometimes difficult, or when everything was not perfect, was to keep reminding myself, "Well, I chose it."

If I could go back and do it all again, I probably would not be the same mother I was back then. From the very beginning, I would have started creating an environment in which my children were encouraged to talk in more open ways. I wanted to be a really good mother, but I was a product of my own upbringing, and my parents were quite strict. I tried to be strict with my children because I thought that was the way a good parent should be, but that wasn't my natural way. I was trying to be conscientious, but I think I should have stepped back a little. I could have listened to them more. I loved them—I always did that—but I could have encouraged them, starting when they were really little, to know what they were feeling and to express themselves openly.

I think that I would have been warmer and more demonstrative in showing love to them. My mother was a traditional Norwegian mother. Norwegians are known to be cool and not affectionate. My mother wasn't particularly warm or physically affectionate, and I think that was passed on to me. I loved my children deeply, but if I could start over, I would show them more. I would say "I love you" more and be more demonstrative with love, hugging them more than I did, so they would really, really, truly know how I felt.

I would also enjoy my time with them more. We should enjoy each and every moment. Love every minute you've got, all the way through, babyhood on. Treat each day as a gift. That's what I've learned we should do, and I didn't always do that as a younger woman. I took things so seriously. I think that you need to *enjoy* the process of raising children because your kids are with you for such a short time. You don't realize at the time what a short and important time you have in their growing process. I didn't know that then, but I think that's what I do now: I enjoy life thoroughly.

Julie's high school graduation photo, 1972.

Becky's high school graduation photo, 1974.

Family Vacations

Every summer, Bob and I planned a family trip. I loved those family vacations. We'd take a couple of weeks off, fill the car with food, pack up the family, and head north. We often stayed in cabins on lakes, where we'd cook most of our meals, but we also sometimes ate out. The kids remember those trips with great fondness.

One of the summers when the kids were in high school, in the early '70s, we decided to go way up to Canada and stay on Lake Winnipeg, which was gorgeous. The kids remember that beautiful lake with the most gorgeous sand. Before we went, I had read that Queen Elizabeth II and her family were going to be traveling through Canada at that time. Secretly, I wanted to see her because I've had a love of English literature and history all my life. The queen is exactly my age, and her children are about my kids' ages. On the day that the queen was scheduled to visit Winnipeg, close to where we were staying, I said to my children, "Let's go see Queen Elizabeth." The kids weren't interested. They didn't have the same feeling for her as I did. But eventually, I convinced them, and we all went into Winnipeg and got there just as she was approaching. I climbed up a tree, so I could look out at her because the sidewalks were so crowded. From my perch I could see the queen, her husband, Philip, and two of their four children passing by in a coach. A hush fell over the crowd when she went by. Everyone was in awe. That was one of the most exciting moments in my whole life! The kids all thought it was a good experience, too, even if they at first hadn't wanted to go. They were very happy after they saw her. They didn't know it had been my secret plot all along to see the queen!

On a different trip, we went to the North Shore of Lake Superior, and the kids remember the beauty of the woods in northern Minnesota. (In fact, I love it so much that I took two trips there after Bob died. I spent a week there one summer, and then the following summer I spent a week canoeing up there in the boundary waters. Joel took a similar trip.)

Throughout the years that the children were growing up, we often got together with Bob's brother, Jim, his wife, Esther, and their children, Jane Ann, Karen, and Lois. Joel especially remembers spending time with his cousins. One 4th of July weekend, we met Jim and Esther and their children at Lake Minnetonka and stayed with them in a huge house that they rented. We spent our time fishing, swimming, and sitting on the dock by the lake. My kids remember having sparklers for the first time there. They also remember going to the science museum, where they saw an Egyptian mummy. Jim and Esther's children are about the same age as our children. Once, while we were staying with them in a cabin in northern Minnesota, Becky wrote a letter to Grandma Anne (Grandpa Vic had recently died). She wrote, "Dear Grandma, we are having a wonderful time. We had a tornado last night, and Lois fell in the lake." We all still laugh about that.

Holiday Traditions

ON HOLIDAYS, WE USUALLY SPENT some time with Bob's family and some with mine. We had the Geisendorfers over for Thanksgiving every year, and we went to Marion's at Christmastime. We went to see my folks on the farm at Round Lake, and my sisters also lived nearby. We often had family over to our house for backyard events in summer.

Our church had a program on Christmas Eve each year. Then, on Christmas Day, we would go to Marion's to celebrate with the Geisendorfers. Marion and Wes's home in Luverne was about 30 miles from ours in Worthington. We'd drive there during the day, and Marion would serve a big meal. We always took Grandma Anne along with us. The kids developed a kinship with the Geisendorfer side, and they still have that feeling of closeness.

We spent Christmas night with my side of the family. Mother and Dad still lived with their big collie in the house that I grew up in, and the whole Wilson family would gather there on Christmas night. My mother did all the cooking and baking for this event. She would go all out every Christmas. The kids still remember their grandma's wonderful egg coffee, which she made in her big coffeepot. (To make egg coffee, you mix eggs—shells and all—with coffee in a big pot and bring it to a boil. After it boils a while, you strain out the eggshells, so all you have left is the wonderful, golden-colored coffee.) Her coffee had such a wonderful aroma. The children also remember the delectable aroma of my mother's homemade bread. She always baked a round cinnamon bread, which she'd slice and serve topped with Cheez Whiz and a stuffed olive. And for Christmas, Mother always baked all kinds of cutout cookies. She made bell-shaped cookies, frosted in red, and Christmas trees, frosted in green and red. She would have a great big spread of meat—mostly summer sausage. Every year she made creative gifts for each of her children's families. She chipped wood on plates and decorated them or cross-stitched big pictures. My mother decorated her tree with candy canes, and everyone got one when they went home.

During the festivities, the kids had the upstairs to themselves. All the cousins made lots of noise jumping on the beds, shouting, and running from room to room—the boys chasing the girls, and the girls slamming the doors so the boys couldn't get them. Mother said the noise didn't bother her a bit because she was hard of hearing. The kids remember those family gatherings with fondness. I liked being there with my siblings and their families, and Bob got along very well with my family. Some of my siblings lived farther away, so they couldn't always be there, but everyone who could come did.

Losing Grandpa and Grandma Geisendorfer

Bob's dad died not long after we moved back to Worthington in 1961, and after that, Bob's mother lived all alone in her home. It was really hard on her. We would take Anne to church every Sunday, and she'd sit with us. After church we'd bring her out to our home to have a meal. She was fond of her grandchildren. This lasted for seven years, but when I started working full-time, I just could not do that anymore. After that, we took turns with Bob's sister, Marion, having Anne over on Sundays.

Anne stayed in her own home until about 1965, and then she moved into a high-rise senior development in Worthington called the Atrium. When she became unwell, we moved her to a nursing home. She died soon after Bob and I moved to Forest City, in 1981.

Losing My Parents

My dad kept farming as long as he could. When he decided to retire, he divided his 640 acres into three separate sections. He sold the part with the homeplace to John Vihlen, a young man who was a neighbor. He sold the second part to Jerald, my oldest brother, who later gave it to his son John. And Dad sold the third part to my brother Gordy. Gordy changed a township road that ran through his portion into farmland. He had previously bought another farm south of my dad's place, so he had a homestead there.

After they sold the farm, my parents moved into town in Round Lake. Dad just hated living in town. They moved there in March of 1968. Three months later, in May, he got sick. He was sick one whole week, and then he died of a massive heart attack on May 27, 1968. The next day, the *Worthington Daily Globe* ran a piece about my father under the headline "Prominent Man Passes." At his funeral, the pastor said, "Jake was a man ahead of his time."

Jake and Geneva Wilson in their later years.

After Dad died, Mother decided to move to Worthington. She rented a place in the Intown Apartments and lived there for a while. She started going with a man named Henry Sampson, and on a dark Sunday night in December 1973, they had a car accident. They weren't wearing seatbelts, and Mother crushed her larynx. She was treated at a hospital in Sioux Falls, South Dakota, and then she was moved into a nursing home. She survived for seven more years. She never regained her ability to talk, but she was a very strong woman and very bright. While she was in the nursing home, she wrote a book about her life (see appendix). She died there on December 2, 1980.

*"Be strong and courageous. Do not be afraid;
do not be discouraged, for the Lord your God
will be with you wherever you go."*
Joshua 1:9

Chapter Eight

Returning to College

For the first 10 years after becoming a mother, I didn't think about going back to teaching because Bob did not want me to work. He wanted me home, taking care of the children and the household. But then, in the 1960s, right around the time when Joel was approaching school age, I started getting offered part-time positions in the local school system. We were in a small community where people knew me and knew that I had taught school. I wasn't applying for jobs; I just got offers. By then, the public schools required full-time teachers to have a bachelor's degree, which I still didn't have. But with my two-year certificate, I was qualified for part-time positions.

But Bob said no. He did not want me to go to work. Then in 1966, when Joel started 1st grade, I got yet another job offer. I said to Bob, "I am going to take this job because it won't hurt the children to have me gone when they're in school. And I'll be home when they're home." At first he was concerned because he thought I might neglect my household responsibilities, but when he realized that my working benefited all of us, he changed his mind. I explained to him that I would not be leaving the family. That's what was important to him.

I started as a substitute teacher, and then I got a job working one-on-one with children who needed help in reading and math and who qualified for services under the federal Title I program. I held this position part-time for about five years. Going back to work was not a challenging transition for me, especially because my kids started helping a lot more around the house. I was very pleased that they were so efficient in the household.

After I'd been teaching part-time for several years, I decided I really wanted to apply to teach full-time. But first I needed to complete my four-year degree. And that meant going back to college.

Even though I'd left college after earning my two-year degree, I'd never given up on my original goal of earning a four-year degree. After we got married, Bob didn't really care to have me go back to school. But by this point I was determined to go back. I talked it over with Bob. At first, he didn't want me to go. After some discussion, however, he agreed that it was a good idea. He could see that having me work full-time would help us pay our bills. When you've got three kids planning to go to college, you need money. I'd had such a hard time finding the money to pay my own way through college, and I was determined to help our children pay for college as much as possible.

Plus, this was in the 1970s, and the expectations for women's lives were starting to change. Women were joining the workforce, and most families needed two incomes. In the end, Bob agreed that, if the end result was that I would take on full-time work, I could go to college. So I went.

In 1970, I enrolled in Mankato State's off-campus courses. The courses were taught by Mankato State professors, but they met in Worthington, so I didn't have to leave town. Classes were held in the evenings and on occasional Saturdays, and I took as many classes that way as I could. Then the following summer, I enrolled in a six-week summer session on campus in Mankato, which is about a two-hour drive from Worthington. Since it was too far to commute, I stayed on campus during the week and went home only on weekends. Leaving the family was stressful, but I accepted the fact that I was doing something that I should do. Once I got on campus, of course I loved it. I was torn between college and my family, because I loved both.

Once classes began, I became excited by the challenge. I absolutely loved college. I loved everything about it—the whole works.

It's not easy to explain this, but I think a love of learning is just in my genes. As you watch children develop, it becomes evident that we all are born with certain innate proclivities. Some people have musical potential, which I did not have. Others have artistic talent, which I do have. I also was born loving to learn, and because I loved it so, I became a happier person while attending college. I was just so happy for the privilege of pursuing my education. I had it all: I had a husband. I had the family that I wanted. And I got the college education I'd always yearned for. This was what I really wanted!

I took classes on campus for a couple of summers. During those sessions, I was free to immerse myself in my studies. One session I took 16 credit hours of classes (the average student takes eight) and earned A's in all my classes.

While I was away, Julie and Becky helped run the household. They were both in high school by then, and they became quite capable of taking care of the house and cooking. They did a beautiful job cleaning—when I'd come home on the weekends, the house was spotless.

Earning My Bachelor's Degree

It took me five years to earn my degree, but I stuck with it. In 1975, I graduated with a bachelor's degree in Education, English, and Speech. I'd so enjoyed college that I didn't want to leave. My advisor recognized my potential and told me, "You should get your master's degree." I came home and told Bob what my advisor had said, but Bob said, "No way. If you don't need a master's degree, you're not going to get one." He didn't want me to consider grad school because he knew it would mean more time away from him. In retrospect, I'm glad he discouraged me. It's not good to leave the family. And I didn't have to have a master's at that time to teach in the school district, so I chose not to continue.

After I had my degree, I was offered a full-time teaching job. Even though Bob had felt hesitant about me returning to college, he was really happy when I started working full-time because I was able to contribute to our finances. Bob appreciated that I was working and was very pleased with me. He would brag to people about me getting my degree. He thought that was quite an accomplishment. And because he was very proud of me, I was pleased with myself.

*"A new commandment I give to you, that you love one another:
just as I have loved you, you also are to love one another."*
John 13:34

Chapter Nine

The Children Grow Up

After the girls graduated from high school, they both went on to college. Julie went to St. Cloud State University to become a teacher, and Becky went to nursing school at St. Mary's University in Minneapolis. Following her graduation in June 1976, Becky married Wayne Henkels, whom she'd met in high school. That same summer, in August, Julie married Joel Lorenz. (Becky's marriage to Wayne ended in divorce. She later married Eric Sitarchuk.)

Joel was still in high school at the time, and Bob and I had a real good time at home with just him. Joel liked to cook and make breakfast. And he went on several trips with us. We went way over to beautiful Mackinac Island on Lake Michigan. Only bicycles are allowed there; you can't take cars. The three of us went all around Lake Superior. Joel and I both loved hiking, so we took him out west to some of the national parks. We went to beautiful Lake Louise in western Canada. While we were there, we went up into the mountains, where there was still snow.

Joel's high school graduation photo, 1978.

After high school, Joel attended Worthington Community College. In 1981, he married a girl he knew from high school, Jill Bohning. After they graduated from the community college, they moved to St. Cloud, and Joel continued his education up there. They did not have children, and their marriage ended in divorce in 1988. (Joel later married Shamese Rutherford.)

Bob and Lola in their backyard in Worthington, circa 1976.

Becoming Grandparents

In 1977, Bob and I became grandparents when Becky and Wayne's daughter, Nicole Marie, was born. We all were very happy about that. Becky and Wayne were living in Minneapolis at that time, so we got to see them a lot.

In 1979, Julie and Joel's son, Aaron, was born. They lived in Worthington, so Bob and I were right there. The following year, in 1980, Becky and Wayne's son Robert was born. And then in 1982, Julie and Joel's daughter, Lisa, was born. In 1987, Becky moved to California. She was pregnant at the time and delivered her youngest son, Ted, in September of that year. Bob and I visited them out there, and Bob just loved that. All our grandchildren were born when Bob was alive, so he got to meet them. Sadly, he didn't live long enough to meet any of our eight great-grandchildren. (I also have three step-grandchildren: Shamese brought to her marriage with Joel her daughter, Tiana. And when Becky married Eric, he brought his two children, Jack and Lauren, from his first marriage, to the family.)

Being a grandparent is different from being a parent. You don't have the same responsibility you have for your own children. You can just enjoy them. When Aaron and Lisa started junior high, I invited them for lunch once a week, and they could invite a friend to join us. That continued until they graduated from high school.

Bob and Lola with grandchildren Robert, Nikki, and Aaron, 1980.

Lola and Bob with granddaughter Nikki, 1977.

Bob and Lola with Nikki, 1979.

Lola and Bob with grandchildren Aaron and Lisa, 1982.

Tiana, Joel, and Shamese, 2008.

Shamese and Joel, 2010.

The Children Grow Up 89

The Wilson siblings at the First M. E. Church in Worthington, circa 1980. Top row, from left: Stan, Woodrow, Jerald, Doug, and Gordy. Bottom row, from left: Lola, Barbara, Julane, and Carmen.

The Wilson sisters, circa 1980. From left: Julane, Barbara, Lola, and Carmen.

Three of the four Wilson sisters, 2010. From left: Barbara, Julane, and Lola.

Moving to Forest City

In May of 1980, when Bob was on a business trip to Greeley Gas Company's headquarters in Colorado, he found out that the company had been sold. Bob wasn't going to be able to stay with the company in Worthington after the takeover; he had to find a new job. All summer long he got offers for various positions, but he didn't take any of them. We didn't know what we were going to do. I had to tell the school administration in Worthington that I might not be teaching there the following fall.

Bob, circa 1980.

Then, on a Friday in August, Bob got a call from Peoples Gas in Forest City, Iowa, asking him to apply for a position. We both went to Forest City that week, and he applied. The following Sunday, 10 days after their first phone call, the folks at Peoples Gas called to offer Bob the job. They wanted him to start work right away.

I didn't want to leave Worthington. I was teaching 3rd grade at Central Elementary School. I liked my job, and the principal of my school wanted me to stay. But Bob wanted me with him, so I went, and I'm so glad I did.

When we first arrived in Forest City, I looked for a job, but there were no teaching opportunities for me at all. I did a little subbing, but I had to find other ways to fill my time. It was an adjustment for me, going from teaching full-time to suddenly having so much free time on my hands. Bob was busy with his new job, and I didn't know a lot of people. Even though the people I met in Forest City were friendly, you don't get included in existing groups right away.

Before leaving Worthington, I had taken a watercolor class. The instructor had told me, "Lola, you first have to know how to draw before you learn

Lola and Bob's home in Forest City, Iowa.

to paint." So when I moved to Forest City, I started taking private drawing classes. I also took watercolor classes at the University of Iowa for two summers. I was developing a whole different side of myself, something that had been sleeping for many years. It was a side that had always been there, but I hadn't realized my potential because I'd never had the opportunity to cultivate it. I also started piano lessons.

Bob got along real well in his new job. He liked the people in Forest City, and they all liked him. After he died, the office girls took me aside at a Christmas party and told me what a wonderful boss Bob had been. They said, "We didn't work *for* him, we all worked *with* him."

Bob really appreciated having me move with him, and he wanted to make me happy. When our dog, Heidi, died, Bob found another dog for me—a miniature collie that we named Meggie. We bought a lovely home, just like one you'd dream about. Bob said, "Lola, it's the house you have always wanted." It was on a cul-de-sac in a friendly neighborhood. Almost right away, we made friends with our neighbors. In the morning, we would have coffee together, and we'd gather together to talk in the evenings. Because we lived on a cul-de-sac with no traffic, we would have big picnics right out on the street in the summer. It was a wonderful, social neighborhood. Every spring and fall, my neighbor Alice Jollivette and I took a wildflower book to East Prairie Park and identified flowers. She and I walked many times by the Winnebago River, which flowed near our homes.

When we got to Forest City, Bob offered to join any church I chose. He said, "Lola, because you joined the Lutheran Church for me, you can join any church and I'll go along with you." I went all over town sitting in the different churches—Presbyterian, Methodist, all the different ones. I chose to join the Immanuel Lutheran Church, and we went faithfully every Sunday. There, we met an older couple, a pastor and his wife; she took me under her wing and invited me to Bible studies. I got acquainted with people and became real active in the church.

On the weekends, Bob and I traveled all around Iowa to different spots of interest. We both grew to love it there. We went to a Norwegian-American heritage museum called Vesterheim, which is known for its collection of *rosemåled* trunks. I was so taken with the Scandinavian art of *rosemåling* and so inspired by the trunks I saw at Vesterheim that in the winter of 1983, I started taking *rosemåling* classes at night in Forest City. I painted and decorated a large trunk for each of my children in the traditional Norwegian style.

In the winter of 1982, Bob won a trip to the Bahamas, and I got to go with him on a cruise. That was great! Gorgeous water and sand!

The years that Bob and I had together in Forest City were wonderful. By then, we'd grown a lot together and learned to accept each other, despite our different temperaments. He learned to accept that I was a messy person. That was hard on him at first. And I'd learned to accept his perfectionist ways. I did my part by working hard to try to keep the house in order, but it wasn't easy for me. (They say all artists are messy. I don't know if that's true.)

Chapter Ten

Losing Bob

In the summer of 1988, Bob's health started to deteriorate. He felt weak. The doctor he consulted told him that he should have mental health tests. He thought Bob's problems were all in his head, that it wasn't a physical thing. But Bob disagreed. He said, "That's not right. I really don't feel well." He was getting very, very weak. He and I had always liked taking walks through the parks in the area, and suddenly he couldn't handle walking very well. Mason City, Iowa, had a reputation for having good doctors, so we decided to get an appointment there. He underwent a thorough physical examination and scheduled a second appointment for the next week to go over the results of the exam. We were scheduled to return to Mason City on July 5. Sadly, the day of that appointment, he died.

The night before, on July 4th, Bob complained of a headache and asked me to put some cold cloths on his head. I did that for him, and he said, "Don't move, because I want to get to sleep. If you move around a lot, I can't get to sleep." When I woke up the next morning, it was so quiet in the room. I went around to his side of the bed to check on him, and he was gone. He had died of a massive heart attack. I called the hospital, and then I called the kids. The kids were very upset that the doctor had told Bob his problems were all in his head, because they absolutely weren't.

We had two funerals, one in Forest City and one in Worthington. Pastor Ole Winter conducted both services. Bob and I had had a wonderful, supportive marriage, and people recognized that. After he died, a woman who owned a beauty shop near us in Forest City said to me, "I was so envious of

Lola and Bob, in one of the last photos taken of him, 1988.

you two, how you got along so well." We did have a good marriage, and I feel very fortunate to have had him in my life for so many years.

After Bob died, it was really tough. I couldn't think properly, despite how I tried. I was completely on my own for the first time in my whole life. Bob had always been very helpful to me, and we made a good pair. Now, all of a sudden, I was alone. People in Forest City were very kind to me, but I couldn't talk to anyone. If I tried opening up about my true feelings, they'd say, "Oh, that's okay. You'll get along; you're doing well." One thing I did that helped a lot was join Stephen Ministry, a program in which laypeople provide care for others who are hurting. I went through the training and became a Stephen Minister. They say that when you are hurting and you help others, you also help yourself. I've found that to be true.

Finding Faith

MY FAITH HAS BECOME MORE important to me in the years since Bob died. I didn't have a lot of faith when I was younger. I attended church, but most of what went on there just went over my head, as it does for a lot of people. That's the way it was. I would sit in the church, but I wasn't experiencing true faith.

After Bob died, all our neighbors came to see me to offer their condolences. But there was one neighbor who kept to herself. Then one day about two months after Bob died, she knocked on my door and said, "Lola, I want to talk to you." She told me that she knew what I was going through because she had lost her first husband. "Lola," she said, "the most important thing that you have when somebody dies is your faith. Never let go of that! Hang on to that!"

At first, I didn't really understand what she meant by that, but I appreciated her advice. She had unselfishly shared something with me that was important to her. She had the consideration and kindness to tell me how she felt; not everybody does that, and she did. I took her words to heart.

After that conversation, I began a long process of developing my own sense of faith. It's hard to explain. Through the years, it gradually developed. Faith doesn't come all at once. It takes time, like anything good. I started reading from devotional books every single day. That helped me grow through the day, and then at night I would review my day. I'd done that a little bit before but on a more superficial level. Now, something started to change. And through the years, every time I would get blue, I would say to myself, "Lola, hang in there! Hang on to your faith!" My faith now is the most important thing in my life.

"Let not your heart be troubled; ye believe in God, believe also in me. In my Father's house are many mansions; if it were not so, I would have told you, I go to prepare a place for you. And if I go and prepare a place for you, I will come again, and receive you unto myself; that where I am, there ye may be also."
John 14:1–3

Chapter Eleven

Living on My Own

After Bob died, I felt I should move back to Worthington. I would have liked to stay in Forest City, but I couldn't see a future for myself there, all alone. Julie was in Worthington, as were several of my brothers and sisters. I still owned our old house there—we'd been renting it out for 10 years—and that was one more reason that it was wise to move back.

Before I could move back, I first needed to sell my house in Forest City. While it was on the market, I started looking for a job. There were no teaching jobs, but I was acquainted with quite a few people at Waldorf College in Forest City, so I applied for a job at the library there. I immediately was offered a position, and I worked there until I moved back to Worthington and even afterward for a while. I loved working at the college, and I met delightful people. I had some interesting experiences: I supervised study groups for the football players, and I tutored a girl from Laos (she couldn't speak a word of English) for one year, so she could transition into a classroom the following fall. I also tutored her mother.

My house in Forest City was very hard to sell, but three years later, in 1991, I finally got a buyer. My former neighbors tell me that it's been in good hands and that it's still beautiful. Just around the time the Forest City house sold, the people renting my house in Worthington gave notice that they would be moving by May 1st. I sold the Forest City house, hired a mover, and moved back to Worthington.

I loved working at the library in Forest City, but after I moved back to Worthington, the commute was too much, so I started trying to find work closer to home. I did some substitute teaching. Then I worked at the County Art Center, and I liked that very much. For a while, I taught English as a Second Language (ESL). I also helped with new student registration for a number of years.

It felt good to be back in my own house and in my church. Still, it was an adjustment, just as anything is. Because my love is art, I started taking art classes at the local college in watercolor, drawing, art appreciation, and art history—the whole works. Those kept me really busy. I took piano lessons from Pastor Bob Knutson's wife, Rita. I'm not very practical, so my brother Jerald took me under his wing. He guided me, because I needed help. He passed along different tips, such as, "In the winter in Minnesota, you should always have a lot of gas in your car. Never get low." He told me where to go to get new tires. He was there for me. I don't think I would have handled everything as well as I did if it hadn't been for him.

Hank Funk and Lola. Date unknown.

I never really thought about getting remarried. It would have been too difficult. It took Bob a while to adjust to me, and a second husband would have had to adjust to a lady who was pretty set in her ways. And I would have had to adjust to a new man. I did have a good male friend for many years named Hank Funk. I met him in the winter of 1993, when my brother Jerald invited me to accompany him on a bus trip to Chanhassen, Minnesota. Hank was a retired farmer from Reading and a very nice man. The two of us had lots of fun together going out to eat, traveling, going to the movies, attending concerts here in Worthington, and participating in family gatherings. I liked his family. Neither of us wanted to get remarried, so we remained just good friends. He passed away on February 7, 2016, and I miss him.

A Sampling of Lola's Homemade Christmas Cards

FOR MANY YEARS, I HANDWROTE Christmas cards in which I recounted events of the year, often illustrated with small drawings or photocopies of pictures I thought the recipient would enjoy seeing. It was a creative joy to make these cards (often on legal-sized heavy paper), which I sent to friends and family.

Lola's 2005 Christmas card.

SEASONS GREETINGS 2000

The year 2000 was a year of Great Trips for me! In March I visited Alaska (Joel lives there). The picture on the top left shows a view from a chartered plane over Denali National Park over Ruth Glacier. We did not land! In July & August visited London (American Council for Educational Studies Theatre Trip). Included were: Romeo & Juliet, Tower of London, had tea at Kensington Palace, saw the changing of the guards, Bath, Stonehenge, Globe Theatre, Oxford University, Canterbury Cathedral, and MORE! Oh, yes, loved the National Art Gallery. In October I was running down the beaches of Sanata Barbara! (CAL) Becky and Ted (Gr.7), Robert At University in Santa Barbara, and Nikki Cal Poly, San Luis Obispo. In Nov. I visited Forest City. If I missed anyone hope to see you next time around! Now home, I will spend Christmas with my family here..Julie, Joel, Aaron at the University of MN, Lisa, a senior in high school. I take piano lessons and continue to watercolor and active in church and MORE!
I hope you all have a blessed holiday season and the year 2001.

Love,
Lola

Living on My Own

Hog barn built by Lola's father and mentioned in Lola's 2000 Christmas card.

Christmas 2000 with love, Lola

The hog barn built by Jacob Oliver Wilson in 1920..Clover Leaf Stock Farm, Granada, MN. When I go on Interstate 90, past Fairmont and I see the sign that says "Granada exit", I often stop by the place where I was born and look at this building which is still standing and in very good condition. It's huge! It's awesome! I look around the place and it all brings back fond memories of my childhood there. One of my Christmas memories! Mrs. George Tonne, our neighbor to the east, made fancy decorated cut out cookies every Christmas. They hung on her Christmas tree throughout the Christmas season. She then invited me to her home after Christmas to share them with her along with milk. So then after Christmas I would trudge across the frozen fields to the Tonne house and we two would sit in her kitchen with the cookies, milk and good conversation. Then I would walk back home, usually was late afternoon. Sharing my memories for me and for all of you with this picture. If anyone would like one on hig her quality paper in either watercolor or colored pencil, please let me know. This letter is also to remind all of you of the WILSON GATHERING THE LAST Sunday in July at the Expo Inn in Worthington.

CHRISTMAS GREETINGS 2003

One of the joys of this season is hearing from all of you. I look forward to this every year. To update you on my family and me. I enjoy my piano lessons, watercoloring, knitting, reading, church (Bible studies, Release time). My goal is to exercise more! My one big trip this year was to go to Boulder, Colorado to visit Nikki; and we also saw Ted and Becky. Julie and I drove out together. We stayed at Pat and Ron Lorenzes.

Julie teaches in Fulda. Joel farms and is active in community. Aaron is doing graduate work at IA State University, Ames. Lisa is a Junior at Augustana College, Sioux Falls, Sd. A music major, also in liturgical dance.

Becky lives in Santa Rosa, CAL. She works as a nurse at the San Francisco University hospital. In the picture you see her right before her accident on the ski slopes at Lake Tahoe. Last winter. Involved her thumb..tearing the ligaments off the bone. Something like that! Ouch!
Nikki..A biomedical engineer working in Boulder, Colorado.
Robert..graduated from U of Cal., Santa Barbara, last year, applying to law schools.
Ted..tenth grade, works as a caddy, loves to snowboard and golf.

Joel married Shemese Rutherford last December. Her daughter, Tiana, is eleven years old. She plays the violin. The whole family love the out of doors in Alaska. Shemese and Joel work in hospitals in Anchorage.

Wishing you a blessed Holiday season and a blessed 2004.
Lola

Travels

In recent years, I've traveled a lot. Julie and I traveled together to Alaska twice to visit Joel and Shamese. We went to Denali and Seward, and we went halibut fishing out in the ocean, where the waves were high and rocked the boat. I visited Becky when she was living in California quite a few times and also in Philadelphia, after she moved there. I've been to Holden Village in the state of Washington. I've traveled to Nova Scotia, and I've been to England twice. The first time I did a Shakespeare tour with a high school group because my granddaughter told the instructor about my love for English literature. We went to Stratford-upon-Avon to see one of Shakespeare's plays, and we went to London. I also went as a chaperone with the Waldorf College band to Germany, Italy, and Switzerland. Two summers ago, Julie and I fulfilled a dream and went to Norway. We started in London and stayed in the Grange City Hotel on the Thames, near Tower Bridge. From there, we took a Princess cruise to Southampton and went along the coast of Norway. We visited Olden, Skjolden, Bergen, and Stavanger and saw the fjords. We had a fabulous time eating fantastic food and meeting unforgettable, wonderful people.

I love to travel. I think what I love most about it is meeting all kinds of people whom I never would meet otherwise. Of course I love the scenery, too. It's both. Travel satisfies a need. Getting out of your regular environment is an exciting adventure. I feel fortunate that I can break out of the ordinary.

Actress for a Day

ONE INTERESTING EXPERIENCE I HAD that stands out in my memory is the time I was an extra in a movie. I was visiting Becky in California, and she was working as a stand-in in the filming of a movie called *Getting Even with Dad*. She asked me, "Mom, would you like to be in a movie?" I said, "Yes, I would like that!" We went to San Francisco to see if I could get chosen as an extra. The movie crew picked out clothes from my own suitcase for me to wear, and I got in line with other hopefuls. To audition, we had to walk through the streets of San Francisco. I was afraid to get out of line because I didn't know my way in the city, and I was afraid I might get lost. I was worried that everybody in the line would move too fast and leave me behind. There I was in the big city. Where would I go? I was scared to death, so I hurried up to be right in front by the leader.

When I got to the front of the line, the woman who had picked out the clothes for me motioned to me. "Come, follow me," she said. I followed her into a bus depot. The movie starred Macaulay Culkin and Ted Danson, and the two actors were standing right in front of me. The woman said, "You cannot talk to either one." I was behind Ted all morning long as an extra in the movie. I didn't do any acting; all I had to do was stand there, right behind them. The crew fixed my hair and covered up my white t-shirt. They told me how to move and that sort of thing.

Getting picked for that movie really surprised me, particularly because I'm a plain-looking person. One of the other women who tried out to be an extra showed up looking really fancy. She kept asking me, "How did *you* get that part?"

I ended up in the final movie. You didn't see much of me, just my hair and me moving around, but it was a fun experience for a woman like me, a woman who lives a very quiet life. Not everybody from the Midwest can say that they've been in a movie!

Being a Great-Grandparent

STARTING IN 2010, MY GRANDCHILDREN started having their own children, and I became a great-grandparent. I have eight great-grandchildren: Harper, Nicholas, Julian, and Aris (Aaron's children); Caleb (Lisa's son); and Ewan, Cara, and Anya (Nikki's children). Tragically, my granddaughter Nikki was diagnosed with Stage 4 breast cancer when her youngest child, Anya, was just seven months old. After undergoing extensive surgery and chemotherapy, Nikki died on December 15, 2017, at age 40. The loss has been terribly painful for everyone in the family, in particular for Becky and for Nikki's husband and children. I think about Nikki every day.

Nikki and Ed's wedding, 2004. Top row, from left: Aaron, Ted, Ed Nikki, Robert, and Lisa. Bottom row, from left: Julie, Becky, Lola, and Joel.

Nikki with her husband, Ed, and children Ewan, Cara, and Anya, January 2016.

The Lorenz family, circa 2014. Standing: Joel, Lisa's husband, Nate, and Lisa. Seated: Julie with Harper on her lap, Aaron's wife, Alexis, with Nicholas on her lap, and Aaron.

Lisa, Nate, and their son, Caleb, circa 2016.

Alexis and Aaron with their children, Aris, Harper, Julian, and Nicholas, 2017.

Because some of my grandchildren live far away from me, it has not been easy for me to see them in recent years. I used to travel out to California to see Nikki, Ted, and Rob, but it's become harder and harder for me to get out there. I would like to have them closer to me. I have been able to develop a closer relationship with Aaron and his family because he lives in St. Paul with his four children, and with Lisa and her family, because they live in nearby Sioux Falls, South Dakota. I get to see them over the holidays quite a bit.

Lola and her "California family," winter 2015. From left: Eric, Ted, Cara, Ed, Nikki, Ewan, Lola, Becky, and Rob. Photo taken in front of Hank's Creekside Restaurant, Santa Rosa, California, when Nikki was pregnant with Anya.

In April of 2017, right after Easter, my three children and some of my grandchildren and great-grandchildren visited me in Worthington to celebrate my birthday and my sister's 100th birthday. Some of them traveled great distances to be here. Joel came from Alaska; Becky and Eric came from Philadelphia; Robert and Ted came from California. Nikki and her family were scheduled to come. They had their airline tickets and hotel and rental car reservations all set, but Nikki was in the throes of battling cancer and was not doing well, so they unfortunately had to cancel. But except for Nikki and her family, everyone else was here.

Joel, Becky, Julie, and Lola, 2011.

My Life Today

In February 2018, I celebrated my 92nd birthday. I can't believe I am 92. I feel good; I don't feel like a 92-year-old woman. Goodness, I feel very thankful for that! I'm very thankful for the good genes I inherited from my parents. My health is good, and my mind is still sharp. I'm particularly thankful for my mind because I see people whose minds are going, and that's one of the saddest things that can happen. Good health is a precious gift.

I don't think we should put all people of my age in one box and say, "Oh, she's 92, and that's the way she is." Every one of us is different. There's no reason that I would be like another 92-year-old or that they would be like me.

My eldest sister, Julane, is the only sibling of mine still living. She turned 101 on February 12, 2018, and she lives in a nursing home in Worthington. She's doing quite well, health-wise. She still participates in many activities, and that helps keep her mind active. Of course, I miss my other sisters and my brothers, and I miss Bob and all the other people I've been close to in my life who have passed away. But I'm enjoying this stage of life as much as I can. I still live on my own in the same house in Worthington. My family is what's most important to me, so of course it upsets me very much that I don't get to see my children and grandchildren and great-grandchildren who live far away. Fortunately, Julie and her husband still live in Worthington, and I appreciate them, but I wish I were able to spend more time getting to know my grandchildren and great-grandchildren who live so far away. That's the thing that makes me feel the saddest. But I can't expect everything to be the way I want it to be. I remain actively involved with my church and community. I have a busy life, and that's a good thing.

About 12 years ago, I took a position on the First Lutheran Church's staff as a parish visitor, and I'm still in that role. I also participate in Bible study at my church. I'm a member of various groups in the city. I belong to PEO International, a women's organization and sisterhood. I study with the 8:30 Club, a group of women who study various topics of interest together. Currently, we are studying the presidents' wives. I'm scheduled to give a talk on Mrs. Monroe, the wife of President James Monroe. I also belong to a widows' group. Another special group I belong to is called the Round Lake Red Hats. Many of the members of that group are women I've known all my life—original Round Lake townspeople and people from the country whom I knew from my time in 4-H. It's fun to talk with the people I knew when I was 12. We say, "We had fun when we were 12, and we're having fun now!" It's nice to visit together.

I still nurture my artistic side: I've continued with my watercolors and done quite a bit of knitting. I was invited to join an art club. There are about nine members of all different ages in the group—some are just out of high school, some are in their twenties. The leader gives us an assignment, and then we create whatever we want. The last topic was to put a person in a place, so I painted myself, surrounded by leaves, so fall will never go away from me. In April and May of 2018, a watercolor painting of mine was exhibited in the Nobles County Art Center in the Area Art Show.

I continue to read a lot. Instead of watching TV, I read. I subscribe to several magazines: the *Smithsonian*, the *Atlantic Monthly*, the *Economist*, and *Vogue*. (Amazingly, *Vogue* has wonderful articles. They feature some far-out fashions, but the articles are excellent.) I've never stopped learning and growing. The librarians all know me because I'm at the library all the time. I'm part of a book club that meets there. We meet once a month and share our opinions and thoughts about the selected reading. I just love that and feel very blessed to be a part of it.

I take Tai Chi classes every week at the Center for Active Living. I started Tai Chi about three years ago. The instructor lived in Japan for seven years, and she became certified there as an instructor. It's a wonderful activity. I gain a sense of well-being by participating. All the different movements strengthen the mind, and it just makes me feel alive.

BETH RICKERS/DAILY GLOB

Lola Geisendorfer (from left), Worthington, applies paint to canvas while art instructor Bobbie Alsgaard Lien gives some pointers to Sharon Lemley, Worthington, Wednesday during an oil painting workshop a Minnesota West Community and Technical College Worthington campus. Several of the participants braved the chilly spring conditions to paint directly from the landscape at the college.

Clipping from newspaper showing Lola painting. Date unknown.

Chapter Twelve

REFLECTIONS

I was born into this life with certain personality traits and natural abilities, but I'm also a product of all the different experiences and relationships I've had throughout the years. I've grown and changed continually. Many people helped me grow in my life—my parents, my siblings, Bob, my children, and others.

What is most important to me is my faith and my love for my family and for the people around me. Finding faith was a transformative experience. I look at people in a different way because I realize they're all God's creations. I watch people and try to imagine being inside their skin and how they feel. I'll go visit a person in a nursing home, and when they tell me, "I have had a bad day," I can understand how they feel. When they share a part of themselves with me, they become a part of who I am, and I become a part of who they are.

As the years have gone by, I have become more comfortable with myself. When I was younger, I sometimes was self-critical. I maybe wished I was more like somebody else. It's important to be comfortable with ourselves the way we are, accepting our faults and recognizing our assets. As we get older, I think we realize that there are some parts of us that we can't change. They say that, to a certain degree, a child is born the way they are going to be. I learned to accept that I started life with a certain personality and to be comfortable with that. The wise philosopher Socrates said, "Know thyself." You have to know what moves you and what matters to you. Discover yourself, because nobody else can do that for you.

As we grow older, we also learn to more easily accept change in our lives. As you can see, I've lived a long life and endured a lot of changes. I've moved around quite a bit and had lots of different life experiences, and I've been grateful for them. You learn gratitude. You don't always have that when you're young; you take things for granted. When you grow older and look back on your life, you're thankful for the many people and experiences—even those that weren't always good—that helped you grow.

One of my favorite passages in the Bible is John 13:14: "A new commandment I give you—love one another." My advice for my grandchildren, great-grandchildren, and future generations of our family is to *love* people. Through all my years, I've realized love is the most important thing. Love of everyone—love of family, friends, and even people who seem unlovable. Learn to go through life looking at everyone you encounter with a sense of love in your heart, and it will change your entire life.

Chapter Thirteen

Afterword

Five weeks before my mother passed away at age 92, she seemed healthy and energetic. She was active at church, leading a Bible study group, visiting congregants confined to their homes or a care facility, attending her weekly art class, preparing her own meals, and driving herself around Worthington. Cognitively, she was as sharp and intellectually engaged as ever.

Then the week before Mother's Day in 2018, she took a tumble in her garage and apparently sustained some internal injuries. She didn't tell us that she had fallen, I suppose, because she didn't want to worry us or make us wonder if perhaps she shouldn't be living alone in her house any longer. The following week, she came down with what she thought was a stomach virus. She suspected food poisoning. When her condition worsened, Julie took her to see a doctor. Within a week, we learned that she was suffering from advanced ovarian cancer and had injured her lung, probably in her fall. She could have received treatment for her cancer, but the odds of it working to stem the progression of the disease were slim to none.

Mom was clear-eyed about her condition and her options. She chose to forgo treatment and asked that she instead be kept comfortable for whatever time she had left. She faced her situation with remarkable strength and dignity. We arranged to move her from the hospital in Sioux Falls to a nursing home in Worthington where she could receive hospice care. It was the same nursing home where her sole surviving sibling, her sister Julane, lives. Always a lover of nature, Mom requested a room with a view. She spent her final days gazing out the window at the beautiful trees and birds. Her room was just down the hall from Julane's.

Julie and her family were there, and Joel and I flew in from our respective homes out-of-state to see her. For a couple of weeks, a constant stream of visitors flowed in and out of her room. Her pastor stopped by almost every day. People from the church popped in along with her fellow artists and neighbors.

Fortunately, Mom was never in pain. She stopped eating, but she was awake and alert. She was even enjoying reading the copy of Homer's *The Odyssey* that Joel brought to her when she was in the hospital. She gradually became weaker, and on June 22, 2018, she peacefully slipped away.

Mom's funeral was held in her church in Worthington. A large group of relatives and friends gathered to remember her and celebrate her life. Julie read scripture, and I created a slideshow of family photos. She would have loved the send-off we gave her.

Mark Twain once said, "I do not fear death. I had been dead for billions and billions of years before I was born, and had not suffered the slightest inconvenience from it." That thought makes sense to me, and I like to think that Mom, being the voracious reader she was, would appreciate his humor.

Becky Sitarchuk
August 2018

Lola Mae Geisendorfer

Lola Mae (Wilson) Geisendorfer, age 92, of Worthington, died on June 22, 2018 at South Shore Care Center in Worthington, MN. She was born to Jacob and Anna Wilson on February 16, 1926 on a farm near Granada, MN. Lola graduated from Round Lake High School and afterwards attended teacher training in Blue Earth, MN. She worked in several country schools when she first started teaching (Rushmore, Reading and Ocheyedan). Lola received a Bachelor of Science Degree from Mankato State University in 1975 for Education, English and Speech. She was a teacher at Central Elementary from 1975-1980 until moving to Forest City Iowa. Lola married Robert Geisendorfer on August 20, 1950. She remained active throughout her life, participating in art groups, PEO, tai chi and other activities. Lola was a faithful servant to many churches including First Lutheran Church (Worthington) where she was the parish visitor, assisted with youth programs, children's sermons, teaching her women's circle and was on the Evangelism Committee. Lola selflessly donated countless hours of her time to the love and care of others.

Lola is survived by daughters, Julie (Joel) Lorenz and Rebecca (Eric) Sitarchuk and son, Joel (Shamese) Geisendorfer and sister, Julane Coyer, four grandchildren, three step granddaughters, eight great-grandchildren.

She was preceded in death by her parents; her husband, Robert, in 1988; two sisters, Carmen and Barbara; five brothers Jerald, Gordon, Stanford, Douglas and Woodrow, and one granddaughter, Nikki McKenna who recently passed in December 2017.

Memorial services will be held on Saturday, July 14, 2018, at 11:00 a.m., at the First Lutheran Church in Worthington, MN, with Pastor Jeanette McCormick officiating. Family burial will be in the Worthington Cemetery.

Memorials are being collected for First Lutheran Church and ARK Enrichment Program for Harmony Elementary School (1935 Bohemian Highway, Occidental, CA 95465) and can be made out to the Nikki McKenna Scholarship Fund. This program was initiated by Lola's late granddaughter, Nikki, and thus, honors both Lola's family and her love for teaching and learning.

Benson Funeral Home in Worthington is in charge of the arrangements.

The cover of Geneva's personal history.
The appendix reprints the text of the original booklet.

Appendix

GENEVA

March 19, 1890–December 2, 1980

This is the story of Anna Geneva Peterson Wilson, our mother. When she was 85 years old, we asked her to share her life story with us. We urged her to write what she remembered from her long and busy life.

When I was reading what our mother wrote about preparing her notes for printing, I realized that a lot of the writing was grammatically incorrect and often thoughts rambled. However, I decided it was best to leave the story "as close to Geneva's story" as possible.

Carmen Lillian Wilson Jones
Editor

January 1, 1975

This is a New Year's Day in Worthington, Minnesota. My birthplace was on a small farm about one-half mile from a small town of Clermont, Iowa, Clayton County. The date of my birth was March 19, 1890.

My father's name was John C. Peterson and mother's was Thora Nelson. My father's and mother's folks came from Norway and bought some farmland two miles east of Clermont. There were 14 children in my father's and mother's home (my father being next to the youngest). They had a beautiful farm home, and were fairly well fixed as their home was lovely. My father's parents died when my father was about 8 years to 10 years or maybe younger. One of my father's other brothers joined the Civil War. One day before my grandparents passed away, my father and his mother were out on the front porch. They saw a white horse and a man riding the white horse. My grandmother said to my father, "They are bringing us bad news about Gilbert." He was killed in the battle of Chattanooga, Tenn. That was the way they received the news of my uncle Gilbert's death during the Civil War by a messenger riding a white horse over the hills. Uncle Gilbert was one of the other children.

My father's parents died while Father was rather young. He and uncle Chris were to make their home with Rears. Mr. Rear was married to my father's sister. They did not live long with them. They did not get to attend school, but only a few months a year. At an early age, my father left and found work for himself so he must have made a living. Later, he and my mother married.

My mother's father and mother were both from Norway and born in Norway. This was my grandfather's third marriage. He had some relatives in America that wanted to come here to make a home. There were four children in the family. My mother was six weeks old and she had a twin sister. There were three older children. There was one son. His name was Torkel. My grandfather died as they were coming to America so my grandmother was left with five young children. He was buried at sea. So there was my grandmother left alone to come to a new country. She had some relatives who helped her. She bought a farm near St. Olaf, Iowa. She farmed the land and raised her family. Her son Torkel bought the farm when he was old enough, but my grandmother lived on the farm until her death. She raised her family well. She had a room built onto her home because now

Torkel was married and she wanted to be by herself to do her own work. She lived on her farm until her death.

My mother was a very talented person. She could do most every kind of work. When my father and mother were married they lived on this little farm which my father had bought. There were four in our family. Henry, my brother, Mary and Bertina were my sisters. My father liked to farm but this farm was not a good farm. It was hilly, stony, and a creek ran through the land. We had a happy home. My father was a studious type. He studied in his spare time. He did not get to attend school much but he decided to help himself in books and reading. I was the youngest one in the family for six years. During this time, I was with my mother and father. We called them, "Mamma and Papa." The older ones went to Clermont Public School and a Sunday School class on Sunday in Clermont.

We were members of Clermont Lutheran Church. That is about two miles from Clermont. It was an old church, but it is still going strong. We were baptized in that church. It is a brick church. When Bertina attended school in Clermont, she must have been about in the fourth or fifth grade. The teacher told Papa that someday Bertina would be a teacher. I spent much time with Mamma. She used to herd cattle and I would be with her. I also walked to town with her. I was the baby of the family for six years. Papa had many pet names for me, but they were in Norwegian. We talked Norwegian in those days. We had a good home. Mamma was such a clever woman. She taught me the Lord's Prayer in Norwegian and we knelt at our bedside before going to rest for the night. I remember walking to church with Mamma. Papa was a hard worker. He farmed well, but he wanted a larger farm and better land, but Mamma did not want to move to a new country and leave her brothers and sisters. We had an old house but plenty of room. Every room was carpeted. Spose Mamma had cut and sewn the strips together. It was all homemade. Even our kitchen and dinette had carpeting. In our parlor bedroom she had made a big shelf. Around the shelf, she had made a trimming. It was wide black velvet and painted flowers with bright colors. On this shelf was Mamma's and Papa's big pictures—one of each of them. Around the shelf was the black velvet with colored flowers tacked on the shelf. I did not mention it, but my mother and twin sister were only six weeks old when they came to America and losing their father as they were coming here. That was real hard life for my grandmother.

We had a good home. Mamma and Papa were kind and loving parents. I spent my first six years with them. The other ones went to Clermont

Public School. I was not old enough to attend school. We had close neighbors and plenty of fun for growing youngsters. We were a happy family. I cannot remember any quarreling among us youngsters. My mother was a lover of flowers. I can remember the beautiful hollyhocks which grew by our parlor bedroom windows. They were taller than the windows. I cannot remember so very much as I was quite young. On Christmas time, we always had a good Christmas. I remember Mamma buying and making things for Christmas. This she would put away until time for Christmas. I remember where she put the gifts. They were hid on a shelf in our bedroom. We were not supposed to know and I cannot remember but we never looked to see what was up on the shelves.

I spent the first six years of my life on a small farm which my father owned. I do not remember any pets which I had. But we had a female dog which I loved. She gave birth to a litter of pups. Papa could not keep her because of having too many dogs so he said that he gave her to our uncle who lived near Elkader, Iowa but they put her to death which I did not know at the time. But Papa let me have a puppy. I named him Bob. He became one of the family. He protected us, later no one dared to come near us. He was not safe for strangers unless we were with him. Bob lived with us for a few years. We have been living together— Mamma, Papa, and sisters, Mary and Bertina, and Henry, my oldest and only brother. We were a happy family and did not know what sadness or grief was. Papa was kind and so was Mamma. This was the first six years of my young life on the small farm near Clermont, Iowa, Clayton County.

In the spring of the year 1896 we four children were taken ill with German measles. We were quite ill and Mamma took care of us. She had not had the measles and now she was expecting a baby in April. We recovered well from the measles but then became ill with the sickness. A little son was born and he lived only a few days. He was baptized Elmer. Now Mamma was seriously ill with the measles besides having a baby. I do not know how long she was ill but she passed into her eternal home on April 12, 1896. We were all by her bedside. She was passing into Heaven. She saw Angels. My aunt was singing Norwegian hymns when she passed away; a wonderful death but sad ones were left here behind. She died in our Parlor Bedroom. Brother Elmer was buried in his mother's arms in the same burial casket. They were laid to rest in the East Clermont Cemetery. My mother was in her thirties so she was still rather a young person and would have had many years to enjoy her family. But God knows what is best. She had Faith in her Lord. On her deathbed, she did not realize what was left behind. She entering Heaven where no sorrow or sadness is felt. I cannot remember too much about after the burial but I remember seeing Mamma's hats and dresses but no Mamma, but we children played together and Papa tried to be a good Papa which he was. We always said Grace before eating and always remembered our prayers at night. We knelt by our bedside as we said the Norwegian Lord's Prayer. Papa was a very temperate man. He used no tobacco of any kind and no liquor was ever touched by him. We girls as we became older remembered those things. We should not even go with young boys who had liquor on their breath. Our mother's prayers were always with us. When we went and did something wrong, we thought of Mamma's prayers. They are with me yet, and now I am 85 years of age.

Papa was a studious type of a person. He did not get to attend school only a few months during the growing years. When he became older, he studied himself. He read good history books and all books which would help him. That was his hobby, to study. I can remember Papa working at arithmetic problems, and he helped us too when we needed help.

Now our family life has changed. Mamma and Brother Elmer are in Heaven where there is no more grief or sorrow. I wonder if she knows what we are doing.

Papa had now to keep hired help in the house. We were too young to do any work and the oldest went to school. I don't remember what I did, suppose I would be with Papa, or play with the neighbor children. In the fall of 1896, Papa took me to Beloit, Wisconsin to spend the winter months with my mother's great Aunt. Papa took me on the train to Beloit. She lived in town in a large house. She was alone. She had one son, I do not know what his work was, but I remember Gilbert coming home to see how his mother was. I do not remember what I did during the time I stayed in Beloit. But I remember Papa came back to bring me home again. How happy I was to see Papa. I would not let him out of my sight. I clung to him. He took me back home with him. I remember getting back to our own home. I wore long dark dresses and pantaloons. My front teeth were gone. That was my age of losing my baby teeth. I must have looked funny to my sisters and brother. They laughed so at me. Bertina said that I had dozens of dolls. I went behind the door and cried but it was soon over. We became friends like sisters and brothers should be. Our home now has changed, I do not remember too well about many things. All our relatives lived here or not so far away. We had very close neighbors and they were good to us, motherless children, but Papa was kind to us and tried to be a good father to us now when Mamma was not there anymore. He played with us when possible. Grandma Nelson stayed awhile with us after Mamma was gone, but she was not young anymore so she went back to her own home near St. Olaf, Iowa.

Now Papa wanted to sell his small farm and go west to better farming and more land to work because we were growing up too, and needed to learn to work. One day Papa sold his little farm. The buyer wanted the place and house the way it was, so now we were soon out of a home. He bought the furniture and everything except our clothes. My mother's and father's big pictures we could take, also a dresser which Mamma had bought before her marriage. It was an oak dresser and also my pet dog named Bob. He was sort of an angry dog to strangers, but he was a God send to us motherless youngsters. He would not let strangers get near us. Papa must have left to look for a new home. He wanted to go west where farming and livestock was a better place for his family. It was not easy for Papa. He was yet a young man. Good in every way. Honest as the day is long and tried to teach us to be too. During the time when Papa was gone, I stayed with our neighbor who lived just across the creek from my homeplace. Henry went to stay with Aunt Annie Anderson. She had a son of Henry's age. They became good friends. She was a widow. She and her older girls helped her farm. Mary went to stay with our Aunt Rierson. She was my mother's living sister and she had a daughter of Mary's age. They became close friends and cousins. She had a wonderful good home. Bertina went to Cousin Bertina Rear Houg. They lived on a beautiful farm home near Elgin, Iowa. Bertina Houg was Bertina Rear, my father's oldest sister. She was a wonderful person. Mr. Houg lived with them. He was a father-in-law to Bertina Houg. Oscar Houg's father lived with them. This was his former home and farm. It was a beautiful place, a lovely yard, beautiful trees and a beautiful big house with all kinds of lovely furniture. Bertina Houg was a very loveable, kind and thoughtful person. She believed in the best things that this world could offer. Bertina had good training while she lived with them. That is why Papa wanted her to have a good training before leaving our home, friends and relatives, and going out amongst strangers and a new country. Bertina Houg had 2 sisters, one was Julia and Bertina Houg had Bible reading, hymns, and prayers every morning. She taught Bertina how to make bread and tried to teach her how to prepare meals. Sister Bertina would be our housekeeper when we went to our new home.

Papa had gone now looking for a new home. He was gone several months. When on his trip he bought a larger farm, 160 acres, good soil and good farming. It was a farm 7 miles west of Forest City, Iowa, in Winnebago County. Now we would be moving away about 150 miles west of Clermont. It was more a farming country. Not so rocky, hilly and creeks. Then we got ready to leave our home, friends and relatives.

Papa had a covered wagon all fixed, so we could take just a few things. Trunks for our clothes, 2 big pictures of Papa and Mamma. Our dog Bob had to be with us. Papa also bought a lovely team of black horses. They were young and just beautiful. They were black and shining. One was named Prince and he sure was a prince for beauty. We had another young colt leading behind. He had a bad hip and Papa took him with us. I named him Grant. I felt sorry for him because he could not jump and run like the rest of the team. Our cousin Henry Rear went with us. The Hougs, where Bertina stayed, were the most wonderful people. There were 3 girls in that Rear family, Bertina, Julia, and Emma. Bertina and Emma had taught school. I do not know where they received their education. I'd not known much about that. Emma was a good singer. She played the guitar and loved to sing to Papa and he loved Emma so very much for her singing and playing for him. As far as I can remember, we were soon ready to leave, but one day Papa took me to one of our relatives. They wanted to raise me, Papa never said a word about that to me, but when we got to their home I thought something was up. I clung to Papa, I would not let him leave me, and he took me back with him. I have been so thankful to be with my family. I was only a little girl and got to go with them to their new home. We left St. Olaf, Iowa from my Aunt Reirson's place. Tillie cried because now Mary was leaving. They were all good to us. Before leaving our old home, relatives and friends, we kept some of my mother's books. One was the New Testament. Printed partly in Norwegian and the other half in American. When I became old enough to read the testament in the English, one chapter would be Norwegian and the other chapter in English.

We traveled west there, the town of Charles City. We drove in the day and rested at night. My father always got a place where there was a lady in the house and we would stay at such places. It was along the country road. The men slept in the wagon. It was in the beautiful month of September we traveled west to our new home near Forest City, Iowa. Every day we would travel on the dirt road and rest at night. I do not remember what we girls did, if we walked part of the day or rode on the wagon, and I do not remember where we got our eats, but Papa must have seen that we got food because we were never sick. Now the road is all paved and lovely to travel. In later years we drove over this same road, but now it is much different. It must have taken us about 5 or more day before we reached our new home. We were all anxious to see how it would be. One home where we girls stopped, the lady showed us all her silk dresses. Now we have gone quite a few miles. The country was more level not so many hills like in eastern Iowa. It was a beautiful country all the way. We went through Mason City and Clear Lake. These are the only towns I remember, but I suppose there would be many covered wagons traveling in those long ago day. Going west to a new country, we enjoyed it and think we all did. Papa had now a big load to care for, a new farm and 4 motherless children, but we seemed to be getting along good. Papa always tried to do the best he could. We settled in our new home. It was a good farm, a few low hills and some low places to the tilled. The buildings were all partially new. It was not an old run-down place. The buildings were built on a good place in the center of the farm. It had a new Grove planted. Many hundreds, they were Maple, Cottonwood and box elder. It was a young Grove. The house was small but room enough for us, four rooms down and then enclosed porch and upstairs with one room unfinished, but we used for a bedroom, storing clothes and etc. It was quite a large room and we used it all the time. Henry used it as his room. We girls slept in one of the bedrooms downstairs. There was a barn for horses and milk cows and few other buildings, a big red wooden windmill. The big windmill which pumped the water and a good milk house below the windmill. We loved to climb the windmill and to watch the wheel go round and round. We knew which way the wind was from or the direction of the wind.

We did not have any furniture. The people who lived there were still there they left us a small table. I do not know how we spent our time as we could not go to school. We had no clothes for school or no food for our lunch. There was a country school about 3/4 of a mile away where we belong to, we had close Neighbors. They were good to us. Papa was busy getting the field work done as he had to get more machinery and all. We had three horses in all. Bertina tried to take care of the cooking and Mary and I tried to help. I can't remember any trouble between us children. We got some chickens and more livestock later.

We had a big neighbor farm about one and a half miles from us. - - - T. I. Thompson was his name. He had a beautiful Farm and Home. His place was built on a hill where you could see it for miles. They had three boys. One was Harry. He was about Henry's age and Harry took a boy's devotion to Bertina. She was a sweet girl. They became good friends and later sweethearts and were married— now for 60 years. They lived a happy life. The boys came and spent some time with us. The fall season went quickly then came the cold winter. The only warm room in the house was the kitchen. On winter nights we played dominoes, "Cat and Rat", "Puss wants the Corner", "Hide the Thimble", and when our dad came home in the evenings, we girls used to curl his hair by heating big spikes in the cook stove. He enjoyed that. We had a very good neighbor. They came over and cleaned some for us. Thus we lived alone for a few years. About 1899, my dad remarried to the neighbor girl. She was a young person in her early 20's. She had one son a few months or maybe older. She was a wonderful person. How she could work, clean or do any sort of work. She was a good manager. We were glad to get a new mother. Her son's name was Alfred Jacobson, and she was Marie Jacobson. They were married in March, 1899 by Reverend C. S. Salveson who was later the founder of Waldorf College. They were married at the parsonage in Forest City. Her sister and fiance were the witnesses. My dad and new mother went on a short honeymoon to Gayvill, S. D. Near Yankton, S. D. To visit my uncle Peter.

I must not forget to write about our first Christmas in our new home. We went to bed as usual. We three girls slept together in a bedroom downstairs. This must be in 1898. In the morning on Christmas Day we awoke and found at the foot of our bed each a big paper sack full of nuts and candy. Papa had walked to Crystal Lake about 4 miles after we had gone to bed to surprise us in the morning. We were happy over the candy and nuts. We were invited to our good neighbors for a good Christmas dinner. The rest of the winter we spent in our home. Bertina taught me to read, write and work arithmetic so when I was able to attend school, I was ready for the second grade. Papa and Marie were married in March 1899. Adopted Alfred as his mother was left with a small baby boy by a good for nothing man. My father and our mother visited at Uncle Peter Peterson's home. Uncle Peter was one of the oldest Peterson children. They had a nice home & farm not far from Yankton, S. D. Now they came after a few days visit. Magnus Olson took care of her home while Papa was gone. Now we were happy over a new mother, but she had a big task before her. She was a wonderful woman. The way she could work, baked the most wonderful bread, pies, cookies, very clean in her work. Her washings were as white as snow. Just a rubbing board. No washing machine in those days and all the water had to be carried in and heated on the stove. We all got new clothes. The house was cleaned, re papered and all. Bertina, Henry and Mary started to school. I must have started then, too. Bertina had missed so much school like the rest of us. My new mother worked hard. We did not realize what works she had to do, until we became older. She was a "Godsend" to us. It was not easy to take a mother's place. Now after we became older and married, we then realized what she did for us. We now had a garden, chickens and plenty of good home cooked food. My bread later when I kept house never seem to taste as good as my second mother's did. I got so many pretty cotton dresses. Her sister Johanna helped her with sewing and cleaning.

Johanna was a beautiful girl. She worked some in the Crystal Lake hotel she could do all kinds of work and do it well. We all love Johanna. She was a joy in our young lives. Now can you believe it? One morning here comes the dog which the people took with them. How he found the way was a puzzle for us all. Dad said now Dash can stay if he likes the place so well. He had many miles to travel. He was no good but only a pet. Too lazy to move. Now we had to get rid of Bob my dog. He was getting to be sort of a savage so it was not safe to have him any longer. He was buried in our North Grove. I will remember the place to this day. One dog was enough for us. Now we had a mother in the house. I also had a beautiful flower garden. It was there when we came. It was in part of our garden. Beautiful Lilacs, peonies, a beautiful bed of yellow tame rose bushes. This flower garden was kept for years. My dad planted apple trees near the place. Now our home had changed. We could have girlfriends come and we had good times together. My stepmother was so busy. She taught us how to keep clean and learn to scrub the floor. We had a hardwood floor in our kitchen and we used to scrub that with a brush, soap on our knees. It had to be white as snow and so clean that we could eat on it. When our father and mother were in Gayvill, S.D. to visit my Uncle Peter, their children were more grown up than we were. They had a daughter named Ruth. She was Bertina's age and was like her. She looked like a twin sister. She came to visit us a few years later as she then attended Jewell College in Jewell, Iowa. She became a teacher. She and Bertina were a pair of 2 beautiful girls. Everyone remarked how much they were alike. Must be from the Peterson side of the family. Now we got near to 1900. So many said that was the end of the world but the world is still here.

Johanna went with a wonderful young man. He was a good friend of my dad. He was not Norwegian so Johanna's mother would not let him come and see Johanna. So that was broken up. We felt sad as he was such a nice young man and Johanna was an angel. Now we all went to our country school. It was a one room school. I taught there a few years later. THAT WAS THE WAY YEARS AGO, NORWEGIANS SHOULD MARRY NORWEGIANS.

My dad bought Henry a pony and a 2 wheelcart which had a seat on it. He also gave him a bicycle. Henry was now the age which he demanded things like other boys of his age.

It was now about 1900. On January 2, my mother gave birth to a baby girl. We named her Florence Paulina. Now my mother had 2 children of her own which was very nice. We all tried to help our mother as we knew there was much work to be done. A few months later, I became babysitter for Alfred and Florence. Bertina, Mary and Henry went to the country school. I did too but had to miss many days. There was much work to be done on the farm. My dad was having his land tilled and some building. We had a new granary built. It was a good one. They built an upstairs and a stairway, downstairs was for grain. We had a room built so that it could be used for a bedroom. It was a nice room. Here the hired man and Henry had it for a bedroom. I used to like to go up there and clean and make the bed. They could use it for storing their clothes and etc. Then they could come and go. Now Bertina and Henry started to take confirmation lessons. They went to the Linden Lutheran church, Thompson, Iowa. That was about 5 miles from our place. Henry drove his pony and cart. It was room for two. The church was struck by lightning during a storm and burned. In the fall, confirmation was held in a school house about 2 miles from where the church was. C. S. Salveson was the pastor. He lived in Forest City, Iowa. Henry had a new suit and Bertina had a beautiful new dress. Later she had her picture taken. She still has the picture. Now the years came. Bertina finished the seventh and eighth grade in the country school but later she went to the public school in Forest City. She stayed with my mother's brother and worked for her room and board. She received very good grades in school. I am now attending country school so was Mary. Henry did not care for school. Mary was very quick to learn. She liked the outdoors and could drive a team and ride a pony as well as any boy. I imagine she was good to help our dad with the work outside, too. I now had to help my stepmother. She had much work that had to be done and no convenience to speak of. Not even a decent cook-stove. Later, Dad bought a new big range which we put in the southwest corner of our kitchen. It had a reservoir for water so we had warm water to wash dishes and our faces and hands. Times were hard, but we enjoyed working and helping our folks, and we had our good times, too, with our neighbors young people. We had house parties and would serve lunch, etc. Then some of the neighbors would do the same. The Linden church was rebuilt into a nice church. I do not remember too much about that, but the church is still in use and kept up very nice. Many of our relatives are buried in the cemetery near the church. Bertina was now working for a neighbor. George Halvorson and family. They have 2 sons and Bertina worked there for many summers, so he could get money for her clothes when she went to school in Forest City. She plans to go to Waldorf College later.

Henry, my brother, had gone to the cities to find work. Uncle Chris is living up there. He has a good job as a salesman for a big store. Henry got a job as a street car conductor which he had for many years. Now it was only Mary and I at home now. Dad rented land south of our place 160 acres and now so there will be more field work. (On this morning, it is March 19, 1975, I am 85 years as I am writing this.) Mary and I worked outside and inside. Mary worked all day in the fields cultivating corn by a hand cultivator and walked behind the cultivator. We had no tractors in those days, so the horse had to do the farm work. About this time Johanna got married to a young man. His folks lived near Lake Edwards about 4 miles from our place. Johanna lived in with his family which did not go so good for Johanna. In a year or so they moved and rented a place about 6 miles south of Thompson, Iowa. In the spring, Johanna gave birth to a baby girl, my mother was up there taking care of Johanna as there was no housewives or nurses then get or to go to the hospital. Johanna did not live long after the baby came. She was so sick. I remember her. I was just a teen age girl, but I loved Johanna so very much. I cried so much. Henry my brother said sometime later: "Don't cry Geneva because Johanna was in heaven." She was buried in Linden church cemetery. They could not get a Lutheran pastor so they got a Methodist minister. Was he ever good. I remember his sermon. It was from John 14: "Let not your hearts be troubled, ye believe in God, believe also in me, In my Father's house are many mansions and I go to prepare a place for you. Where I am there will ye also be." John 14: 1-3. It was the most beautiful sermon. It has always stayed with me. Grandma Jacobson and daughter Annie, who was still home, took the baby girl. I do not remember her name when she got baptized, but she lived only a few years. She was buried beside her mother in Linden Church cemetery, Thompson, Iowa. It was another sad death, but such is life. We have to keep going and put our trust in the Highest Heavens. Now it was Mary and I at home. We shocked grains and helped hay. We were busy all summer. Later Mary went a year to Waldorf College and she became a school teacher. A year or two before this, she went to Sioux Falls where Uncle Chris lived. She stayed with them and was baby sitter for their son and also attended Sioux Falls school. I don't think she attended school regularly as she had all the work to do besides caring for Clifford. His wife did not do any work. She took life easy. One summer Clifford came to stay with us on the farm. He was such a cute little boy. When I was 14 years, I started to take confirmation classes for 2 years. Then, when I was 16 years of age, C. S. Halvorson came back and was the minister then. So I was confirmed in the fall of 1906. I sure was glad to get confirmed and get to join the Lutheran church, but it had to be in Norwegian which I did not understand very well. I had forgotten about Norwegian talk and reading. We had to walk to take confirmation lessons, but I enjoyed it as there were other young boys and girls like myself and we used to visit together. I did not mind the walk. It was in the summer time. I had to get my work done in the forenoon because I would have to walk 5 miles and be at the church at 2 p.m.

We had our house now finished with rugs and lace curtains and some new furniture. We always had plenty to eat now. I baked bread when I was 12 years old. We also had many new coats, dresses and shoes. Mary was now going to Waldorf College. Soon she would also be able to teach a country school. Bertina was home teaching our home school. She was a wonderful teacher. Alfred was now old enough to help our dad do light field work. We do not keep a hired man, only when really busy summer comes. Florence and Alfred also had been attending country school. I was confirmed when I was 16 years. C. S. Halvorson was now our pastor. He was a busy preacher. But everyone thought a lot of him, he was a good preacher. There were not so many home now. It made it easier for my second mother. She was wonderful to us 4 motherless children. She saw that we went to school, church and to learn our Bible and get confirmed so we belonged to the Lutheran Linden Church. I still attended country school yet, but I studied at every spare moment. We had good times at our age, too. We used to have basket sociables in our schoolhouse in the winter. Then we would give a program. That was fun to make a good lunch to eat after baskets were sold. That summer I worked at home. I helped milk cows, feed calves, and take cows to pasture every morning and get them. In the fall, I helped husk corn by hand. My mother and I at one wagon. March, 1907—when I was 17 years, we milked 28 cows by hand. Many a time I would milk all the cows and separate the milk and feed the calves. I got to be a regular chore milkmaid, but I did not mind it as my folks were planning to have me attend Waldorf College in the winter term after Christmas. About that time, Ruth Peterson from Gayvill, S.D. came to visit us. She had been attending Jewell College. She visited with us for a few days. She was sister Bertina's age. They were so very much alike. Both handsome girls. They made a nice pair. Enough alike to be sisters. Everyone who they met remarked how much they were alike. She taught school later on, so did sister Bertina.

Mary, my sister, was such a happy girl. She had lots of friends. There were a few neighbors' girls not so far away. We used to walk to Crystal Lake. That is where we got our mail before the mail route came from Forest City, Iowa. I was confirmed in November, 1906. I had the yellow jaundice at the time and was not feeling good, but I got confirmed for which I was thankful.

When my brother Henry was home, we had an old barn which was there when we came. Henry made a bunch of pigeon houses and put them on the south side of the barn. We had pigeons all over. They were pretty, too. Later on, the Barn was torn down. I don't know what became of the pigeons. Henry went to the cities as he became older. He did not care for the farm work. On my 16th birthday, 1906—they had a surprise party for me at Jacobsons, my mother's folks. Their daughter Annie had a birthday the same day. We had a nice party. Annie was older than I was, but the young people came and we had lunch, etc. I was then sweet sixteen as they were called at that age. Don't think that I was very sweet, but that is what they called sixteen (Sweet Sixteen). I do not remember much special that I did, but I worked out, milking cows and feeding chickens as we had baby chicks setting under setting hens. There was no hatchery in those days, or chick feed ready to feed baby chicks. Alfred and Florence were now growing up to be a help. My mother had been very wonderful to us four motherless children, I don't know what would have happened to us, otherwise. She helped us get ready for school and to see we got confirmed, which was a wonderful thing.

For past time, we had house parties. Mary was going to Waldorf College and was teaching about 4 miles from our place. That summer went fast, we were all busy. If we went anywhere we had to walk. We had no buggies then, just lumber wagons and big work horses.

They had a Christmas program in the T. I. Thompson school. They asked me to take part. I was not going to that school. The piece I spoke was: "Little Gretchen" and "The Little Match Girl".

Bertina was attending Waldorf College now again. She worked to get a higher certificate. She must have gone about 9 months. She studied until she got her first degree certificate, which was wonderful in those days. We had a good county Superintendent Brown. He was a good friend of my father. That summer was busy. We baked bread, and canned much fruit and made pickles as we had a big garden. We milked around 20 cows and calves to feed. I also helped feed the young pigs and hogs. I did not care about doing so much outside work, but I planned to go to college soon. I also had to do a lot of herding milk cows. Then I would study, crochet and knit. I learned to knit and crochet. We made lace from sewing spool thread. It was very pretty, but slow work. We would make lace for our petticoats and underwear. No washing machines in those days. We had to carry the water in from the well and wash by rubbing board, and big tubs. It took us all day. My mother wanted the clothes to be white and clean, and to iron, we heated our irons on the cookstove, but we were happy. My mother was an excellent cook. She liked to have people come and eat with us. At Christmas and Thanksgiving, we had turkey or duck or geese as we raised geese and turkeys. The feathers from the geese were put into pillows for our beds. In the spring, March 19, 1907, I was seventeen years old. I had been attending country school until then.

Dad is improving our yard with a fence. Planting evergreen trees. There was a beautiful grove here, but Dad likes evergreens. He keeps the lawn cut and trimmed. We have to help too. There can't be any paper or weeds in the houseyard. He also put in a new basement or cellar. We called it then. It had now an outside stairway before it was in the kitchen floor. One time I fell down into the cellar. There was no railing or anything to hold on to, but I was not hurt. That was when I was a little girl.

I was now 17 years—1907—Bertina worked for our neighbor as she did every summer vacation. Mary was home helping during the summer months. We had now 27 cows to milk by hand and to separate all the milk. Then to feed the calves. One time I was choring alone and it was getting dark, I took the pail of cream by mistake and gave it to the calves. Papa said, "Geneva, you should not have done that." I knew better, too, but it was a mistake. One time my folks left for Britt, Iowa about 15 miles away. They went to visit some friends. I had all the cows to milk at night alone. In the night came a big storm and I was alone. I locked all the doors and slept on the floor downstairs. My folks came back the next day. They went to visit some friends, but I got along fine; I never was much afraid of being alone or afraid of storms.

In September 1907, Mary began to teach. Bertina also taught during the school year. They were both country schools. Henry was away in the cities, conductor on a street car. One place where he drove the street car was to Como Park. How different it is now in the cities after 77 years. I was not home helping my folks because after the holiday season, the winter quarter started at Waldorf College, and I planned to enroll then. Bertina left me money for my room and tuition and I was to wait on tables 3 times a day for my board. In the fall of 1907, I helped husk corn every day. Some - days were snowy and cold. My folks bought me a trunk for my clothes and they bought me my clothes which I needed for school. They made me new skirts and blouses and I also had to have nice dainty aprons for waiting on the tables. They were small ones with ruffles around the edges and of pretty bright color. Well it was the year of 1907 and I was now 17 years old. I enrolled at Waldorf College in January 1907. Bertina gave me money for my tuition and room. I have 3 tables to wait on. They are all young college students and they are very nice to me. My room is on the second floor right near the stairway. We eat in the basement. My room faces north and the girls are all on the second floor and boys are on the third floor. The girls and boys were not allowed to live on the same floor.

In 1972, when Geneva's granddaughter, Janeva, was a student at Waldorf College, Grandma visited the college. How she enjoyed her day. She was able to find her old dorm room and could recall many happy experiences of her days at this college.

If the boys wanted to date the girls, they had to get permission from the lady who had charge over the second floor. I liked Waldorf College. Every morning, it was morning devotion at 6:10, I did not always attend. I thought I should study those 30 minutes, but I found out that I got good grades when I attended the Bible class. Bertina was kind to me, she let me use some pretty blouses which she had sent for. She now had money to spend, I took normal training classes for country school. One day we had to write an essay on Autumn. The teacher or instructor read my essay to the class. She said it was very good and made me happy, too. To be read in front to a large college group. We called the class grammar then. I enjoyed school. We did not go to shows. We were not allowed to attend those 10 and 14 cents movies which was shown 68 years ago. Times have changed now. My roommate was not so fussy who she went out with for a date. She went with the town boys. I would not go out on such dates. I was more on a quiet shy type. In March 1918, I was 18 years of age. I would soon be through with 4 months of Waldorf College. On Sundays, we went to the Lutheran church in the morning, had to be back for table waiting at noon. In the afternoons, we studied or else took a walk if the weather was nice. After 5 months of college studying, I tried to pass the Teacher's Certificate. We had a county Superintendent. His name was Brown. My grades at Waldorf were good, not an A student, but I learned a lot. In July was the time for Teachers training, and also trying to pass the teacher's certificate. It was time for Winnebago Country, Iowa. We spent 2 weeks in training and it was also Chautauqua time which was for 2 weeks. We enjoyed going to that.

Well, I received my third grade Teacher's Certificate on 4 months of college. I could now teach a country school. I got a school about one and one fourth miles from my home. I helped at home. I helped chore, etc. Then, I walked to school to be there at 6 a.m. It was called the T. I. Thompson School. There were only a few pupils—6-8. Not enough to be interesting, but it gave me a chance to start to teach. There were no books or things to work with like there are today. We had to find work for the pupils ourselves. They had a teacher hired for the following year so I was only there 2 months, but I was thankful for that.

Andrew Smith was a boyfriend of my sister Mary. He heard of a vacant school 4 miles, N.E. of Thompson, Iowa. They took me up to see the Director of the school. It was a large school from 20–25 pupils of all grades. He hired me for the rest of the year. I built my own fire in a coal stove, and kept the school house clean. It was a hard school for me. It was a problem because I was new and shy, and quiet type, but I did my best with God's help. I had a boarding place not far from the school; there was not much going on in the community. I did not get to church. If I went any place, I walked. I walked to Thompson, that was 4 miles, but I loved to walk. In the spring of 1909, a farmer passed away leaving his wife and 4 children. She was all alone so she wanted me to come and board with her. Two of her children went to school for me. They were very bright children and good ones. I went and stayed with Mrs. Stanger. She was a very sweet and dear woman. It was so long ago I forgot her name correctly. She kept a very clean house, very good food and I had a very nice room by myself downstairs, where I could put my clothes and take a bath when I wanted to. She kept some milk cows and had some hogs to feed etc. I helped her milk her cows and did all I could to help her. I don't remember if she charged me for my board or not. She wanted me to stay with her for the summer months, but I had to take a Teacher's examination in July and had to think of another school for the coming year.

I got a school that was 4 miles from where I had taught. That was 8 miles N.E. of Thompson, Iowa. I got along with my first year of teaching. The parents and children were very nice to their teacher. I had been home all summer. This school was considered a hard one, too. I got a lovely boarding place. They only had one son. His name was James and he was about 3 years old, a very good little boy. Mr. and Mrs. Charley Halvorson, Scarville, Iowa was where I boarded. It was a lovely place to stay. I had a beautiful room and the food was delicious. She kept a hired girl as she was not well. My school started November 15, 1909. It started to snow early. My dad took me up to my school and place. The snow came about November 13 and never melted. It stayed that way all winter. I walked to school, and built my own fire. Every morning it had snowed in my path, so I had to dress warmer with winter underwear and leggings over my overshoes.

I did not get home until Christmas. It was about 15 miles from my home and our dad had to drive a team and sled. The girls were home for Christmas too. I liked my school and the pupils seemed to like me. They had respect for the teacher. I did not go away much while there. I spent my time studying and working on school work for the children. It was supposed to be a hard school, but I had no trouble at all. At Christmas at the school, we had a Christmas tree in the p.m. as the community did not have any doings at night. The neighborhood was rather rough. We had a program and the parents and pupils seemed to enjoy it. I did enjoy it myself. I was home during the holidays. My dad got the flu, so he had to get someone else to take me back to my school. My neighbor boy took me back. He wanted a date so bad anyway, but I did not care for him, but I was thankful that he made that long trip and was very kind and good.

So now I was back teaching after Christmas holidays. I kept busy studying to get my teacher's grades up. Soon, I would now be 20 years old. Bertina and Harry planned to be married on May 4, 1910. Harry had rented a good farm and he was a very good farmer and manager. Bertina and Harry had been sweethearts since they first met when they were young children. They were married May 4, 1910. Mary was Bertina's bridesmaid and Walter, Harry's brother, was best man. They went to Chicago on their honeymoon to visit some of Harry's relatives. Bertina said it was such a beautiful day. She can always remember the beautiful sunset as they were ready to go on the trip. "I never was so happy in all my life," Bertina said. God was with them. They had a lovely home, and were so happy. They were married at a parsonage.

I finished my second year of teaching. I spent much of my vacation with Harry and Bertina. It was home to me. After school was out, I went to Clermont to visit relatives and friends. I visited the church cemetery where my mother and baby brother were buried. We four children bought a grave stone for the grave. It did not have any words on it. It was a beautiful cemetery and I enjoyed walking through the cemetery, so many of our relatives were buried there. My mother was not very old in her thirties. It must have been hard for her to leave her four small young children.

I attended Teacher's Institute for a few weeks at Elkader, Iowa. I had a chance to teach one month of school not far from our church. I stayed with Bildens. Mrs. Bilden was Emma Houg. They were just wonderful to me. They never charged me anything for room or board. I wanted to pay, but they would not want any. I had some money to spend now as I was about broke. I went back home and got my school again which I had last year, 8 miles N.E. of Thompson, Iowa. I stayed with Clara and Charley Halvorson. She was not well, so instead of keeping a steady girl, I helped in the morning, nights, and on Saturday. I would always mix her bread before I left for school. She said her bread was better when I mixed it for her. I was used to mixing bread as I learned to bake bread when I was twelve years old. On Saturday, I would wash the clothes, then I could get mine washed. I would also wash the cream separator. I loved to help her. She was such a beautiful person, and Charley was a fine man. My board bill was not high as I helped some for that. It was a nice community up there and I liked it. Bertina and Harry are now living in their home. It will be 1 year in May now since they were married. One weekend, Harry came and got me and I fried down meat for Bertina all day on one Saturday as she was not able to stand the grease frying. Once in a while I went out on a date but did not care for some of those dates. They were nice young boys, too. Well I finished my second year at that school. I thought I had done pretty good for me to be 2 years in one hard school, but we go along fine. I made a rule, if no whispering was done during study hour, they would get 100 percent on their deportment. Many worked for that and got their 100 percent on report cards at the end of each month.

Harry and Bertina had now a son born in March. I planned to stay with them for the summer to help Bertina and help Harry milk some cows. Then, during the summer months, Bertina and I took music lessons at Crystal Lake every week. This way I got to learn how to play the piano, as they had bought a new one. I enjoyed taking music lessons and I learned a lot. I practiced an hour every day. Bertina did also. But she knew music a little better than I did.

One music lesson she had was "Sing to Me". It was a beautiful piece. We had a lot of fun over it as we changed it to "Jig me to Sleep" as I went with a boy and he liked to show off and jig and I did not like to see him jig. I guess we mentioned that now, Mary, and Andrew were also married and lived only a few miles from Bertina. Mary was a lovely housekeeper. Everything is so clean and kept in order. This was her first year of marriage. They were expecting their first child in November. They were married last Christmas time. She did not have a wedding. Those days were not big weddings—over 60 years ago. Bertina and I had good times taking music lessons. We drove a team with a buggy top. I helped them all summer. I would help Harry milk some of the cows and wash the cream separator and milk pails and cans. Then we would can etc. It was called the Engleson place. It had a beautiful big house. The men who had the house built for himself and his large family went broke. He lost his farm and his wife left him, so he had plenty of trouble.

Orville was a good baby boy. I helped Bertina with housework, too. The summer months went very fast. I had a few dates with the young man who liked to jig. Every time he came to see me, he would jig as Bertina is a jovial funniness. She changed it to "Jig me to Sing Love". We did not mean it in a mean way because he was the nicest and best young man in the community. He was well educated and good in every way, but I did not care enough for him to encourage him. Bertina and Harry did all they could to make us a couple, but I guess I had my eyes on someone else. Harry helped me get a fall term of teaching about 2 miles from their place. So I still stayed with them and walked back and forth in sunshine and rain. The young man who Harry and Bertina wanted me to have, got married later. He had hard luck. His beautiful daughter died when she was going to Waldorf College and one of his sons was killed on the road by a fallen tree. Such is life. This was over 60 years ago. He has also gone to his Heavenly Home.

I began teaching. It was a very difficult place. I don't know why. The pupils did not seem to realize what school was for. They did not seem to care about the bells ringing at morning, noon, or recess. I did the best I could and did not hear any complaints, I taught there for 2 months, the fall term. They begged me to stay for the year, but I could not handle the boys and girls. So then I was through with that place. I did not have now any school for the rest of the year. I wrote to vacate school which was in Mounty Valley Township, about 6 miles N.E. of Forest City. The reply was open for me so now in early November, I would be starting in a new place. In the meantime, I kept up my studying so I would not have to take a teachers examination every year. I had a few days vacation and went to help Mary. They had a son now. His name was Lloyd. This was in 1911. Now when I'm writing this, it is May 17, 1975. Many years have passed. Lloyd is now a grown man. He is State Auditor of Des Moines, Iowa. He has been for 3 years. He worked his way through high school, Waldorf College and other colleges. Now he is a very good man and even does preaching on Sundays. His mother and Dad are gone. There were 10 children in the Smith family and all did well. I miss Mary, she has been gone for a few years.

Now I had begun my new school in Mount Valley Township. I got a ride to Forest City and from there I had to hire a lively team as there were no cars in those days. I had a nice school. The pupils all seemed so nice. Then, there was also an organ in the school which I could practice on now as I knew some music. I was boarding with a widow, she had 3 boys. It was a good place, clean and nice and she was a very good Christian mother. It was a winter with lots of snow. I walked through heavy snow every morning. We had to burn wood for heating the school room. It was in a good community, too. Nice clean people and good people. I stayed with the widow during the winter months. Then she moved to a small home. I moved with her. It was a nice place and the lady and I had the same room, but we got along fine. I don't remember what I did during the summer months. Harry and Bertina had moved to a larger farm. Harry was a wonderful farmer and manager, so he had the best chance for a young man. Mary and Andrew had moved to Hubbard, Iowa. I now had my teacher State Certificate. I did not need to take an examination now every year. I passed the teacher's state exam and got a life certificate. Now that would not mean much. I also attended 2 months more at Waldorf. The state questions for the certificate came from the state. There were 5 questions in Mathematics. If we missed one, it would be 20 percent off, but I got 95 percent on the exam. I missed only a little mistake so my certificate was O.K. I could now teach in any county in Iowa.

Alfred and Florence were the only ones at home now. So it made it much easier for my second mother. It was not an easy task to care for 4 motherless children because children do not understand the situation a second mother is in.

I was not home much now. Later on, my mother and Dad started a Sunday School in our school house. They had a good attendance. Mother was the Superintendent and Dad was the teacher of the Bible class. They enjoyed these meetings so much. One summer, I went down to visit Mary at Hubbard, Iowa. She had now 2 sons—Lloyd and Harold. Mary was a wonderful person. Everyone liked her and she was a wonderful housekeeper besides helping Andrew with milking and caring and raising chickens. I got a school down there for 2 months. A young man rented a farm about 2 miles from where Harry lived before they moved. His sister kept house for him. She had left her husband and had 2 children with her, Sylverne and Philip. I caught my eyes on this young farmer. He was so jovial and full of life. He like to dance and have a good time. He also played for dances. (violin) I had no dates with him yet. I was not the type to make the first move for talking to young boys. I had plenty of dates with neighbor boys, but I never cared enough to encourage them. I had quite a few chances of marriage, but I did not care enough. My first love was for J. O. Wilson.

He was the neighbor which moved up from Story City, Iowa, and he and Harry became good friends. I became a good friend, that was all yet. I taught only 2 months in Hubbard, Iowa. Then I got the home school. I helped mother. She was not well and Florence was not old enough to do all the work.

J. O. Wilson was the farmer who moved up from Story City, Iowa. He was a young man. He was born in Palto Alto County, Iowa. His father had come from Denmark when he was about 20 years. His wife was a Story City girl. An aunt of J. O. Wilson—Jacob Wilson was his name, but he went by the name of Jake Wilson. His father and mother were married and lived in Marshall Town, Iowa, many years ago. He was a carpenter. There were 4 children in the family. Jake was next to the youngest. When Jake was a baby, they moved to Omaha. Simon Wilson was Jake's dad's name. He did not provide for his family. He used liquor too much and his mother became ill with consumption as it was called in those days. Now it was T.B. She passed away when Jake was about 6 years old. Then Jake's mother's folks came and took the family. Jake went to live with his grandparents (mother and father to his mother). He had a good home with his grandparents. He was baptized and confirmed by them and he also got to go to school. He helped his grandfolks farm the small farm. They lived near Roland, Iowa. When Jake was about 14 years old, his grandfather and grandmother passed away, so now Jake was left without a home. He lived some with his aunt and uncle Ole Larson. They were good to him and they welcomed him as one of the family. He helped his uncle some. They were very good to him and they were very good Christian people and family devotions. Later on as the years went by, he worked for others, too. He liked to husk corn, and every fall, we would husk corn for every farmer who needed help. Corn had to be husked by hand using a corn husker on your right hand Jake became a good husker. He was the Iowa Champion corn husker at that time. One farmer who was wealthy, helped Jake get started to farm. So he started on the farm near Thompson, Iowa. He raised lots of hogs and was good at that. They did not hear from the father after the mother died, for 20 years. Then he came to see his family in Roland, Iowa.

   I taught the home school. That was a snap. The pupils were wonderful and we got along fine. I stayed home with my folks. I did the washing and cleaning on Saturdays. I had dates with some of the neighbor boys. We used to go to dances. One of the boys used to take me to Forest City on Saturday. He had a little pony team. They were as cute as they could be. He was a very nice young man. He lived with his brother on the home place. It was a well built up place, a lovely big, fairly new home. The parents had passed away, one sister was married.

   On Christmas vacation, they had a house dance. My cousin Tillie Rierson and brother Ray were up to visit us. They were from Clermont, Iowa. I think we were at Bertina's and we drove Harry's team. The weather was so cold and wintry. I liked to teach my home school. We had a basket social one evening, we had a good crowd and baskets went at a good price. We also had a program which everyone enjoyed. I finished the school in the spring, and enjoyed the school very much, but I already had another school for the coming year. It was now 1913. Now my brother Henry was planning on getting married to Hannah Paulson, Clermont, Iowa on June 25 at her home. I was to be bridesmaid, and so I got a new white dress made by a lady in Forest City, Iowa. One day I left Forest City by train. I had to stay overnight at a friend of my dad who lived in Britt, Iowa. Hannah met me at Clermont, Iowa depot. It was just a small wedding and Hannah looked lovely. She had a beautiful wedding dress. Nels Anderson (our cousin was best man). Bertha Anderson also went along. We went to Decorah, Iowa. They had their picture taken. Then they went to Minneapolis on a short honeymoon. They then moved into Thompson, Iowa. I stayed in Clermont and Elkader for a few days. Then I came home. They had a new house built on our old home where we lived with our mother, father and we four children. Part of the old house was still in the yard, but I do not remember what rooms they were. It sure looked bleak and lonely. No paint left, but it was old now. It was old when we left it, and when we lived in it, but that was long ago and it was not new then. I always went to visit the Lutheran cemetery where my brother and mother were resting.

I took the train back to Forest City, Iowa. I got a room and did light housekeeping. I was taking sewing lessons during the summer months. J. O. Wilson or Jake Wilson was what he was called by, came to see me on Sundays p.m. I was also attending teachers institute and Chautauqua for 2 weeks. Jake had a lovely driving team and outfit. One of my girl friends said it was the prettiest team she had ever seen. They were not work field horses and he kept them shiny and black and they were dark brown of flesh. Their names were Tip and Tuck. He had raised them himself from a mother horse which he had. Her name was Cute. She was a nice little pony, too. I enjoyed having Jake come to town on Sundays. It was fun driving around in the country. Forest City was a nice little town and the countryside was beautiful.

One beautiful Sunday, Bertina and Harry, Jake and I hired a car to take us to Clear Lake and Mason City. We had a lovely day. Beautiful Clear Lake. We had a boat ride and everything that went on. That was over 60 years ago. I have not been back to Clear Lake, but I imagine it is more beautiful than ever. So many people had their summer homes there. Those that could afford it. I enjoyed my stay in Forest City. The girl friends and I would take walks down to Lime Creek. One was a teacher friend. She went to Waldorf College when I did. I had to sew and press lots of the clothes when we sewed. I learned to press there. The dressmaker was so fussy about that. I sewed until about September. Then I quit because my school would begin soon. Jake was a good farmer. He raised lots of hogs. He now worked 320 acres of land which he rented. That was 5 miles south of Thompson, Iowa.

He was well liked by his neighbors. He was full of fun. He liked to dance and was a good dancer, but I was not, so we did not attend many dances, but he played for dances when he was not too busy on the farm and livestock.

When I was teaching in Mount Valley Township, my father canvassed for sheriff of Winnebago County. He stopped at one of the homes where one little boy went to school for me. My dad told him that I was their son's teacher—the farmer said, "I have never seen any kinder person than your daughter, she is the kindest person I have ever seen." I did not know this until my father told me. This little boy's mother was blind. He was a lively little boy and I had to punish him some, "not much", but when in the wintertime as he was walking home, I saw that he was dressed with his winter coat and scarves and cap and overshoes on before going for home. The farmer said to my dad, she was like a mother to his boy. It was a compliment which I never forgot.

I was now in my sixth year of teaching country school. The wages had increased, so I had put away some money in case I should go to school again.

This school was 4 miles from Thompson, Iowa. It was about 20 pupils, all grades. Charley Halvorson was the director of the school. I stayed with them. This was my third year I had stayed with them, but since they were further north, they had moved. They had a bigger house, a lovely place. Clara was so good. She was a wonderful person. She was such a pretty woman, too. I wish I could be like her, but I had to be the way I was and try to do "God's Will" in my life. James was now a school boy age. He started to school for me. I had about 5 or 6 now in the first grade. Some had gone to school before but still were not able for second grade. I had about 1 mile to walk to school. There were some very talented children in the school. Later on, one became a Lutheran pastor and one was one great teacher at Waldorf College, Iowa.

She was not so young anymore, but she was a second or third grader when she went to school for me. There were a few young people around. Jake came to see me once in a while, but it was quite a ways for a team. A young man who lived near Harry's, got a new car and he would take me to Harry's on Friday evenings and bring me back Sunday. But I was not interested enough to want to go with him. He was a splendid young man. I was kept busy with my school work.

I enjoyed this school very much, Clara and Charley Halvorson were very kind to me, during Christmas time, we had 6 weeks vacation because of cold weather for children to come to school I spent some days with Harry and Bertina and was home for a few days. Then I took a trip to go and see Mary and Andrew at Hubbard, Iowa, but they had moved to a different farm, Mary kept a beautiful clean and polished house. They had now 2 boys, Harold and Lloyd. They are good boys. I got sick at Mary's. I got quincy. That is trouble of the throat. The doctor was out a few times. He wanted to lance my throat because of the gathering in my throat, but it was too close to a big vein and he did not dare to, but God was with me and I recovered very well. So when I was better, I went back to Harry's.

Jake came and took me back to my boarding place at Halvorsons. I went to church with them on Sundays. C. S. Halvorson was the pastor. He had 3 churches, so he was very busy. I had a young boy just in the first grade, but he was such a darling little boy. He brought me fruit and different things. And he liked to be in the schoolroom with me instead of going out to play with the other school children. He was just a precious little boy, always so clean and polite. School was going fast, now this term would soon be over. I might go to summer school with my girl chum, but she said now "Geneva do not go and get married," which I will write later. At the end of the school year, many asked me to come back. The pupils gave me a gift—a lovely mirror, and what else I cannot remember. It was so long ago. Now I remember, they gave me also a lovely jewelry case. I gave it to my daughter. She has it yet on her dresser. It was gold on the outside and silk lining. It was a beautiful box, and is now 61 years old. I went to Harry's and Bertina's. Harry came for me, now this would be the last time I would stay with Clara and Charley. They were so wonderful to me. Bertina and Harry had a baby girl born about April 25, 1913. They named her Thora for my mother and Bertina's. She had her grandmother's name. I worked for them. I did all the work as Bertina was not able to work yet. The baby was only a few days old. In a few weeks, Bertina was up around again, and then we cleaned the house and made the garden.

I had the separator and milk pails to wash as Harry did some dairy. They had a young boy working for them—the weather is getting nice and warm. Oh, yes, now I might get married in June. I had no diamond, but the wedding ring had to be fixed, it was too small. Once when Jake was in Chicago, he bought me a beautiful gold solid bracelet. It was beautiful, Barbara had that, too. Now Jake had not so far to come and see me. I had saved some teaching money so I planned for a piano for one new thing. Lola, one of my daughters, has that (after 60 years). Her girls have learned to play on it. It was mahogany finished. It was beautiful and it is still nice. Orville was a good little boy. He was now 3 years old. Thora was a very good baby, pretty as a doll. They had 2 lovely children, Orville and Thora. We planned to be married June 14, Sunday, 1914 at the Linden Lutheran Church morning services. It would be a simple wedding, but would be in a church.

Sister Florence would be my bridesmaid, a friend of Jake's and his neighbor, would be the best man—Christ Olson. Jake went to talk to C. S. Halvorson about the wedding sermon. I did not go along. Reverend Halvorson asked who was the bride to be. Jake told him. Reverend Halvorson was a good friend to me. Jake told him who the bride was to be. Reverend Halvorson did not say anything for a few minutes. Then he said, "Now Geneva sure is a good girl." He would perform the ceremony after church services Sunday. Everyone was so surprised, but all stayed for the wedding service. I remember Bertina shed a few tears. We were so much together. We told my dad a few days before the wedding, but he did not come to the wedding. I was the last one of his first marriage, he did not like to see any of his girls getting married. I suppose he would miss us. My mother made a good dinner for us. There were not many. Then we drove to Hanlontown, Iowa, and stayed overnight. We drove our team because we did not have a car yet. We had a light lunch at a small inland town (Fertile, Iowa). We had just sandwiches, but they were the best I believe I had ever eaten. We stayed overnight at Hanlontown. Then the next morning, we took the train to Mason City, Iowa for a few days. We bought some good furniture, a dining room and 6 oak chairs, and other things for our living room, a rug, lace curtains, a nice bedroom set. I also bought a piano. These things I bought with the money I had saved when teaching. We enjoyed the short stay in Mason City. Then we took the train back to Hanlontown, Iowa, and stayed with Matt Johnson and then we started for our home. It would be my new home. We drove a team, so I suppose it must have taken most of the day. The corn now needed working, so the men would be busy with that. Our furniture which we bought, would be shipped by rail as there were no trucks in those days. Helen, Sylverne and Philip were there yet. She would sell her furniture and planned to go to Des Moines to find housework, but she did not like it there, so she got a good place near Hanlontown, Iowa. Johnson's got it for her. There was a place where 2 brothers lived. They had a lovely home and everything nice. Their folks had just passed away, so they needed a housewife. Helen was a good cook and housekeeper. She had a good place there—good and sure pay.

The lady where I sewed for one summer, made and planned it. It was white voile long and a slim skirt. The lace was built over the skirt, a beautiful lace and the waist was covered with the same white lace. A satin belt—I should have kept it, but did not because I was too busy with other things. I did not have a veil as they were not used so much then as now. My going away dress was made by a girl at Thompson, Iowa. That was dark blue satin silk and very pretty. It had a pleated skirt. I had lots of compliments on this dress and I wore it very much after the wedding and trip. The length was a walking type.

Recollections Regarding the Wedding of Jake and Geneva

By Carmen Wilson Jones

Occasionally our mother used to talk about her marriage to Jake, the fiddler. It was considered an evil thing in those long-ago days to play for dances. Our Grandfather Peterson was a very righteous man of a high moral calibre and I'm sure that he had many misgivings about his youngest daughter marrying a fiddler. There were also rumors (told to us by the aunts) that Geneva's father had his heart set on C. S. Halvorson for his daughter, Geneva. He was an ordained Lutheran minister and a widower and this would insure a LUTHERAN MARRYING A LUTHERAN. However, as the story goes, when Jake Wilson put down his violin at a country dance (held in a schoolhouse) and asked Geneva Peterson for this dance, then and forever (some sixty years later) it was Jake Wilson for Geneva. Interestingly, the Halvorson family played a part in the Wilson family years later, for in 1957, Reverend Halvorson's son officiated at the ordination services for the son of Geneva and Jake Wilson when Woodrow was ordained into the Lutheran ministry. Also, Reverend C. S. Halvorson baptized six of the children—Jerald, Julane, and Woodrow in Forest City and Carmen, Gordon, and Sanford in Blue Earth, Minnesota.

Now I was a housewife instead of a school country teacher. I had plenty to do, extra men to cook for and wash their clothes. A big house, it was an old house but plenty of room. I fixed up my living room. Now - our furniture was here and it was sure nice. I hung my lace curtains, in the front room. We repapered a small living room and Mary helped me with that. I papered the kitchen alone, it had wainscoting on part of the lower walls, and the ceiling was painted so it was not hard to paper, but it sure looked nice when it was done. I also made curtains for the kitchen windows and later on, I got a new linoleum, which sure made the kitchen bright and clean. I scrubbed the rooms upstairs on my hands and knees so I felt as if it all was clean. The hardest part for me was cooking for so many extra men in busy times. Anna Olson, a neighbor, helped me at threshing time. I could bake bread, cake, and pies. One of Jake's favorite pies was sour cream pie. We had plenty of cream, so I made a recipe by myself. I made a custard from sour cream with egg yolks and white for frosting. Then I baked it. You cannot buy sour cream pie like that now. I went with Jake when I could, but every Sunday, we took a drive someplace. We went to church some, but not like we should have. We could not get along without our church and I sent for a big Bible. I put the names of our family in that. Janeva got the big Bible. Summer was going past and I was kept busy cooking, baking and washing clothes. I washed the hired man's clothes, too. There was no electricity then, so washing was not easy. I carried water in and out and heated it in a big wash boiler on the cookstove. My home was fixed up nice and I enjoyed it very much. I did not miss teaching. In August, we went to the Iowa State Fair, that was part of our honeymoon. Lars was one of our hired men. He kept the house so clean, not a soiled dish left. He must have washed them after every meal. We had a wonderful time at the State Fair. It was the first time I had been to a State Fair. We took the train from Forest City to Des Moines. I do not remember how many days we stayed.

I am writing this today: June 14, 1975, Flag Day—61 years ago since my wedding day, now I am 85 years old and am living in a rest home, lonely without Dad. I miss him so much. So much for then, I will get back to my story.

Now it was getting near fall. Beautiful weather. It was the canning time. I had not done much canning, only helping my mother, but I soon learned how to can. We used an open kettle method as we did not know anything about canning any other way. We did not have any apple trees but there were tame plums. Just wonderful for jam and sauce. I gave Bertina some plums as I knew she liked them too. We had trouble with flies now as we had no fly killers like we have now. Fair time was now too in the counties. We went to see the fair at Forest City, not so much to see but only a county fair. There was always some new thing to see and we could see many people which a person knows or does not see otherwise. Anna Olson, my neighbor, she was good to come and see me, and I walked down there to her place too. She kept house for her brother, Chris. Neither one were married, but Anna had a boyfriend. He was from Norway, too. I think she would go to the cities to try to get housework, as hired help for housework is hard to get now. I was now busy fall cleaning and canning. It soon would be time to put some meat away as corn husking would soon be here. Then it took lots of food as corn huskers get hungry. Philip, Helen's boy, Jake's nephew, was staying with us now. She worked for some boys on a farm near Hanlontown. She could not keep Sylverne and Philip, so she sent Phil to be with us. He was 6 years old or maybe a little older. He was school age and had to be sent to school every day. I was not in favor of having him, but I could not do anything else but to accept it. Philip was not a very strong boy and he missed his mother so very much. I felt sorry for him. He had such terrible headaches at times. I was trying to get him to eat plain food. Mrs. Matt Johnson was Helen's sister. They lived not far from Helen so I thought it would be better for Phil to be with them as they had a boy Phil's age, too, but Jake insisted that he stay with us. He was with us 8 years. He would not like to have me tell him things to do and wear, like going to school on winter days. He had over 1 mile to walk to a country school. I wanted him to wear scarves over his cap, but he took it off and one of his ears became frozen so badly but it healed and turned out O.K.

 We were now busy with farm work, plowing and it soon would be corn husking. I had canned quite a little sauce and now had to prepare meat for meals. We had no lockers and electric help, so everything had to be done by hand. I baked 50 loaves of bread a week, every other day. I could make good bread and home made buns were good. They did not last long. I never bought any bread. They were husking corn now. They had extra men. They stayed here for supper, breakfast and dinner and could they eat. Outdoor air made a person hungry. Now I washed windows and storm windows and took screens down. This house was old like a lot of houses were built in those days. We had finished corn husking and the crop was good. Soon it was Thanksgiving and I suppose we would be home. We moved the piano into a small living room where it was warmer. We had bought a hard coal heater. That was a stove which kept heat all the time. The coal was put in on the top and the stove had flexo glass so we could see the fire. It kept the room nice and warm and we never had to build a fire in the morning. It was self feeding. They do not see those kind now a days. I had also bought a new sewing machine. I enjoyed sewing and playing the piano when I was alone. Winter would soon be here. First winter I was living in my new home. The days go by fast, men to cook for and lots of baking to be done. My sister Mary lived a few miles away and Bertina was also a few miles away. Henry and Hannah now lived in Forest City. They had bought a nice home, it was small, but Hannah had fixed it up so very nice. They had one little girl now. Eldeen was her name. She was a sweet little girl. At Christmas time, Jake bought me an aladdin lamp, they gave good light. Our kitchen lamps were a yellow light. They had to be cleaned every day and filled. Quite a little work with just that. We took our big living room and used it for a bedroom for a few months. It was a nice big room, for we were expecting our first child in late March. We moved our good new bed and now it looked real cozy and nice. The upper stair room was too cold and unhandy to have a baby up there. I made it nice for us to use before the child was here. I had been busy making baby clothes. Something new for me, as Florence was the baby when I was home. She was now about 15 years. Our son was born March 23, 1915. Jake was a proud papa of a son. Now we were wondering what to name him. He was about 7 pounds. He had lots of dark hair, a round face and a very pretty baby boy we thought. Jake was naming him so he would be J. O. Wilson—the second. Jake's name was Jacob Oliver Wilson, so he had to think of some name so we named him—Jerald Oliver Wilson (J. O. Wilson the second).

Jerald was baptized in the Lutheran Linden church. Bertina was one of the sponsors. I was thankful when he was baptized by Reverend Halvorson. Now I knew God's blessings were on him. Anna Olson was working for me and I had a midwife from Thompson for a few days. I could not nurse him as I had no milk. I felt so sad that I cried. So the midwife put him on malted milk. Later on, I put him on cow's milk. I pasteurized the milk and bottles so all would be clean. He seemed to grow, and it was not long before he was a big fat rolling baby. He was a good baby. That summer was a hard one. The summer was cold and it rained nearly every day. Poor corn. It did not ripen, so we had to feed it to feeding cattle. In the summer or spring, Jake became sort of ill. He went to the doctor at Thompson and Forest City, but they could not find anything wrong with him. He was not able to work. I bathed him morning and night. Then in the summer, he went to the Mason City heart doctor. He gave him heart medicine, and he became worse, so he decided to go to Rochester. There they said he was O.K., nothing wrong, but they put him on a diet like cocoa and milk and to bathe him in the morning in cool water and evenings with warm water. It was not long before he was in the gain. I think he had sort of a nervous trouble, he was never bothered anymore. Soon he was just as strong as he ever was, I was always careful how I fixed his food, not too much rich and fried food. We feed cattle so not much corn husking. Times were rather hard now. Jake being sick and poor crops, but the Lord was with us every day. Although we did not thank Him enough. Now I know after years of experience, how the Lord had been with us. Time goes on and we were all busy at something like it was on the farm. I had to pick up fuel for the cook stove and heat all our water for washing and bathing and then I carried it out. Not like today, where we now can press the button and everything is done.

Now the year was 1916, I got sick in January, called and I had a mis- carriage. I guess the year was too much for my strength. Extra men, Phil, and Jerald was a tiny baby, but I was in bed for 1 week. Then the doctor gave me some medicine and I was soon O.K. again. Anna Olson was my helper for a few weeks. She was an angel. It soon was spring again and I raised lots of baby chicks and had a big garden. In the summer months, Phil went to visit with his mother and Sylverne came to stay with me as Helen could not keep the two. They fought and quarreled. Sylverne was about 14 years. She was a very good girl and I enjoyed having her with me. I had someone in the house besides hired men. She was good to help with the work and very kind to Jerald. We could take the team buggy and eggs and drive to town. Maybe Thompson or Forest City. The summer went fast. We were busy. We had a big cookstove and later, I bought a kerosene stove, which made the kitchen much cooler. I got an oven so I could bake on top of the stove. The men were busy in the fields, feeding cattle and raising lots of hogs. We kept 2 to 3 hired men, they stayed with us. I had to wash some of their clothes. I did not do much entertaining company as I was so busy with my work now. Being a new housewife, we had to learn to do things which I never did before, but I enjoyed the farm. There were lots of big trees in the yard so it was nice in the summer. The summer was going fast.

Jerald was growing and doing fine on the bottle milk. He could sit up and he plays. Soon it was Thanksgiving and then Christmas. The men were busy getting the crops and corn in before Thanksgiving. One day before Jerald was born, my folks called to tell me that they had a new baby girl at their home. Florence was now about 15 years so she was a big sister. They named the new girl Joye. She was baptized the same day as Jerald was in the Lutheran Church Linden. They thought a lot of their new baby and was surprised by us all.

It was now 1917, time was going by fast. It was now February and I was expecting a baby any day. We moved our bed into the small living room. It was warmer. It was a cot. I bought a mattress so it made a good bed. Anna Olson was going to help me again. Our baby girl arrived February 12, 1917. It was a cold winter and rooms were cold. My midwife from Thompson came for a few days. We did not have any nurses then. The doctor was also from Thompson, Iowa.

When Julane was 10 days old, she did not have a name yet. But later on, we named her Thora Julane after her grandmother. Jake's mother's name was Julia, but we wanted a different name. My sister's daughter's name was Thora, too, so we called our daughter Julane because there were too many Thoras. Our baby girl was not strong at birth. She weighed only 5 or 6 pounds. I guess I had worked rather hard the last year, we called the doctor and he said that she had pneumonia, and I was not too strong yet, but Anna Olson was there to help me. She was too ill to take the bottle, so I had to sit by the base heater and warm the milk. I fed her with a spoon, but in a few days, she regained her health. I felt as if God was with me. Soon she could take the bottle, but I kept her warm and dry and took good care of her. My mother, when she saw our little weak baby, she said Geneva will never raise her, but it was not long before she was growing. Later on, when she was a few months old, we had her baptized—Thora Julane, but we also called her Julane. She grew to be such a sweet little girl. Everyone took to her, she was so smiling and good. Now I had two lovely children, Jerald and Julane. Jake loved his children. He was very kind to them. He knew what life was without his father and mother. Philip had to go to a country school 2 miles away. It was called District 80. It was a grade school and always there were the best of teachers. There were no lunches in school in those days. We had to prepare a lunch for each child. Now when school was out in June, Phil would go and stay with his mother. Then Sylverne came and stayed with me. She was a good girl. Very good to the children and company for me. Now Jake's dad was coming from California to be with his children here. There were 4 left. Julius was in Roland, Helen and Mattie near Hanlontown, Iowa. He stayed with each one some of the time, but mostly with us. He sure took a lively likeness to Julane. I was sure busy now. We were working 320 acres of land. We had lots of hogs, cattle and some milk cows. That was Philip's work to milk the cows.

Jerald and Julane were growing fast. They were good little children, and I loved to wash and bathe them, every day, especially the babies and always clean clothes. We had a baby buggy which I took along if I took the baby to town. It could be folded and put in the buggy. We did not have any car now or no one else did. Time was going fast. It would soon be 1918. I did not go very much, but Sylverne was there in the summer and she was such good company. We were expecting our third child in March. Now I would have 3 babies, but they were precious to us because God gave them to us to care for. Helen Larson was working for us. She was Jake's cousin from Roland, Iowa. Bertina and Harry had a baby girl born in February. They named her Elaine. My, she was a sweet baby and so good. We had a midwife come out to help, but Helen Larson was a good worker. In a few days, I was up and around, so I could fix the baby's food, and bathe and change his sleeping clothes to a shorter dress vet, Jake's father was with us, so we were a big family with lots of work to do now.

We were wondering what name we should have for our new son. He was a chubby little fun fellow. Now he could laugh and coo. We had to have 2 bottles now as Julane still had hers and if I didn't give her one, she would take our baby's one. Jake's father said we should call our new son Woodrow, so we named him Woodrow Warren Wilson (W.W. Wilson). He was a darling little boy and we all loved him. Julane could not walk when Woodrow was born, she was only 13 and a half months and used a baby walker, but it was not long before she walked and ran all over. Grandpa Wilson worshipped Julane. He babied her so that she got spoiled. Now Jake was restless and wanted to buy some land for his own. I had now lived here nearly 5 years and would also like a place of our own. Soon, one day, Jake and O. B. Anderson, a land agent from Forest City, went to look for a farm. They had good luck. Jake found a section of level land in Martin County, Minnesota. It was 2 miles west of Granada, a small town of about 400, about 7 miles N.E. of Fairmont, Minnesota. This place had been rented out for years. It was not a very old place. It had a big grove all around the buildings, but no trees in the yard for shade.

The main house had gotten burned and the mother, also. The renters were living in a pretty good tenant house. We were now to move in March. We had a big sale, prices were good, so we had money to put payment on the farm which we bought. We paid $120 an acre for it. It needed tilling, fencing and new buildings. We worked at the house first. Julius was Jake's brother, and he was a carpenter as they decided to help. Sadie went along. Now we were a houseful. We moved the tenant house to a nice place in the yard. We built a big cistern and full basement. We had lots of work all summer. After the tenant house was moved, we built a kitchen and bedroom. It was a tenant house which had 4 rooms, 2 big bedrooms, upstairs, and a kitchen in one big living room with a beautiful colonnade between, so it made a pretty room, and we put 2 big windows in the dining area and a big window in the front room. They were on the east side of the house. We also put on 2 small porches. Then we had the rooms papered and some of the woodwork varnished. It was a cozy little house, but not big enough for us all. Julius and Sadie rented a small farm not far from us. We now had 3 small children. There was always plenty to do. Then men were busy tilling and fencing. We built a big hog house and machine shed. We now had a big Buick car. No windows then, but it had wind protection which could be put on and taken off. I used to watch the trains go by. It was not far from our place. The rails were not on the farm, but I could hear the whistle at nine in the morning and about 4 in the p.m. I liked to watch the train go. Fall was going fast, so was winter, but our house was cozy and warm. We got a small heater which burned wood and coal. Soon it was Christmas. We were now about 70 miles from where we lived before. We were not yet acquainted with the neighbors, but they were close by. I liked the place very much. You could see so far away. On Christmas Eve, we had oyster stew and Julius and Sadie were also here. We had a Christmas tree and gifts for each one after our supper. So that was one of our first Christmases up here. Winter was going fast and soon would be spring again. I had lots of eggs to gather and hens to care for. Eggs were a good price. They kept us with groceries and some clothing. On April 12, 1920, another baby girl came to us. God had been good to bless us with 4 wonderful children, 2 boys and 2 girls. We did not know what to name her, but I had the name Carmen thought about before she was born, but Jake wanted Lillian, so we named her Carmen Lillian.

April 12, 1896 was the death of my mother, so now God gave me a baby girl on that date. Now it was April 12, 1920. She was born. She was a darling little girl. We all loved her, and her name was Carmen Lillian Wilson born on the Clover Leaf Stock Farm. That was the name we named and she was born on our farm, the first child born to us there. We all dearly loved our girl. She was plump, light skin and hair. She looked like the Wilsons. Jake thought she was quite a girl. We were really proud of our family now, 2 boys and 2 girls and they sure were a lovely pair. Times were busy as could be on now a new home. We all liked the place. We could see so far and yet neighbors were close enough across the fields. We would go, we had a car now, and I learned to drive.

I am now 85 years old. It is August, 1975. I cannot remember much now to write because I was sick for a while, so I have to get my mind back to work.

Sylverne was helping me this summer. Phil was with his mother while Sylverne was with me. She was a wonderful good help. She did her work well and she was good to get summer along with. I had a big garden. I had men to cook for and separator and milk pails to wash and many baby chicks. I found many eggs every day which had to be cleaned and packed in cases.

We went to Granada, M.E. church. Sometimes they walked and sometimes Dad took us in the car. We did not like to miss Sunday school. I think Reverend Groening was our pastor. He also had Winnebago Church. We all enjoyed our new home. Times went fast. Dad loved his new little girl, and of course her name should be Lillian or Lily Mae, but I had a name already, it was to be Carmen Lillian, which it was. She was baptized, I do not know where, but Julius and Sadie were sponsors. I think we took her to Blue Earth where Reverend C. S. Halvorson was the pastor. He had baptized the 3 others and we felt like he should baptize this one too. Time went fast and we now knew we must join a church for ourselves and the children, so we all joined the M.E. Church in Granada. We were now members of the M.E. Church at Granada. If we couldn't drive the team or car, the children could walk to Sunday school.

In the summer of 1922, a son came to our home. A lovely little son. We had now 5 children, 3 boys and 2 girls. They were well and happy and we loved our little ones. We named our new son Arthur Gordon Wilson. That was after me because I was baptized Anna Geneva, but Gordon now writes his name—A. Gordon Wilson. He was a fine little boy. He had dark hair and dark blue eyes. He was a chubby little boy. We loved him, too. He got his bath every morning, too. I had a girl helping me. She was very good. There was lots of work to be done on a big farm. I had lots of chickens and eggs to work with and care for, but they helped on the groceries and clothing, and we loved our new home. Jerald and Julane walked 2 miles to a country school. It was called district number 80 and they had good teachers, but the teachers were kept busy with all the grades. The teacher had Julane help her with the younger pupils. Julane was so quick in learning. She could read before she started to school. Jerald did well, too, but he was more for the outdoors. We were all kept busy haying and harvesting. In the spring of about 1923, the flu was so hard on some. We got it, the worst fell one me. I could not go to bed because of so much work. I got it so bad, I had to go to bed and then it settled in my head. The doctor came and said that I had to go to the hospital. Dr. Hunt's hospital at Fairmont. It was a mastoid operation. They were serious so close to the brain. I came out fine, but had to be in the hospital for 10 days. While there, when getting better, my thoughts were on the family. I would dream at night that the children were playing around my bed and saying, "When are you coming home momma?", but we had a good hired girl. She took such good care of the children. She took a special interest in Gordon. He was about 9 months then. Mildred Malou was her name. I gained my health back quickly, and on February 23, 1924, we had another son. His name became Stanford Joel Wilson. He was named for his grandfather. Now I was busy. Mildred helped me the greater part of the summer and the children were getting so big, they could play outside in nice weather. Time went by fast. We had now 6 children—4 boys and 2 girls. They were a joy to us. We prayed that we would be good Christian parents to this family.

    In another 2 years, one fair winter day, it was around Valentine's Day, Dad thought he had better go to St. Paul to look for feeding cattle. George Peterson was our hired man. He was a good man. Inside and outdoors and kind to the children. I washed clothes that day, George helped me. I was not feeling good, about 3 p.m. George went to the neighbor lady, Mrs. Niehaus to come over. Then he went for the midwife in Granada. Then they called Dr. Hunt. He came right away and a baby girl was born, a beautiful baby girl, a gift from heaven. She was just like a beautiful baby doll, and we loved her, too. Her name became Lola Mae. The older ones went to country school, and when they came home, they were surprised to find another baby sister. The girls loved this little sister. I told them that we expected a baby and they were old enough to help care for her. Time went by fast and Anderson (Cleo) helped us. She came out once or twice a week and helped wash and clean the house. She was a wonderful help. The girls liked to dress up Lola. We sent for a beautiful little woolen sweater. It was long like a coat and she looked beautiful. She could now walk and talk some. There were no babies now, until 3 years. Then we had 4 girls and 4 boys. I went to the hospital this time. They were old enough to help care for themselves some, and the girls came out to see their new sister. Julane had about 100 names picked out for her, but we named her Barbara Ann. She was a doll and we loved her. They came to see me, and they all looked so tired. We did not have any flowers, so they picked some wild roses to bring me. I cried when they left. I prayed that I would get home to my family, which I did, and they were glad to see mamma. Now we had 4 girls and 4 boys. They were all perfect in health, and we were proud of our family. Everything went on as usual. The boys were now able to run the tractor and help in the fields. The girls helped me in the house. The older ones took 4-H club work. Woodrow won a scholarship through judging, so he had a chance of going to the University Agricultural School to finish his high school work. The Agricultural School was at St. Paul. It was part of the Minnesota State University. Now there is no Agricultural School. It was then a school for high school and agriculture.

The Depression was now here, land prices were not half the price they were when we bought the farm, and farm products had become very low. We now had a hard time meeting extra expenses, taxes and interest on the place in which we now lived and bought. I raised lots of poultry, that helped with our living and clothing. The family was now growing up fast. Barbara Ann was now nearly 4 years old. She was a sweet little girl and we all loved her. Just like the rest of the children. We were now expecting again. On April 16, Easter Sunday, 1933, I went to the hospital at Fairmont. A son was born to us. It was a beautiful day, and Julane already had a name, Douglas Alan Wilson. They were home doing the work. Cleo Anderson came out and helped the girls with the washing and cleaning. I was in the hospital about 10 days. Jerald and Julane went to Granada High School and some went to district number 80, country school. They had 2 miles to walk and they carried a lunch in a pail. There were no school lunches then. Douglas was now the youngest and we now had 5 boys and 4 girls, a big family. He did not gain like the rest of the babies. I guess I was too worked out and too tired to have more children, but we took extra care of him and he soon grew to like the rest. All of the children now were baptized so we are thankful for that. We would soon be living here on. this place 16 years. They were happy years and we all loved the place. But now hard times were here. People were losing their homes and we lost some also. We had put a lot of money on the place, but Dad had a good friend, John F. Haeckel, he was the banker in the First National Bank in Fairmont. He stayed by us and trusted Dad.

Jerald and Julane finished the 8 grades and also finished high school in Granada while we lived here. Julane was salutatorian of her class so she also had a year of normal training in Fairmont. She was the highest in high school. She was now capable of teaching country school. She attended normal training in Fairmont. She was born a teacher—Jerald a farmer. A Prudential insurance land agent man came out to see us about buying land on crop payment. That was just what we wanted to buy. This agent had a 640 section farm 1 and a half miles from a small town of Round Lake, Nobles County. Some lovely fall day, Jake and I decided to look over the farm. It was about 60 miles west of us in Nobles County. It was a big section—2 sets of buildings. It was a good farm. It had good soil and was close to a small town and the children could go to consolidated school and the school bus drove right by the place. Julane was now through with her normal training and was ready to teach country school. Jerald was busy helping his dad with farm work. Jake and I drove over one day to look over the place. John F. Haeckel, banker in the Fairmont National Bank helped us. He gave a good word to the Prudential Land Company for us, so we were now ready to leave our Clover Leaf Stock Farm, friends, and church etc.

Recollections

By Carmen Wilson Jones

The John Haeckel family from Fairmont visited our family often. Our parents were very good friends and exchanged many good meals and fellowship. There were ten children in their family—a set of triplets, Jim, Joe, and Jean. We can recall many lovely Sunday dinners in their beautiful home, also the Christmas packages. Mother would have farm produce while Mrs. Haeckel would have fancy Christmas baking. How we loved those goodies! I recall the first taste of citron in a very rich fruit cake. Several years ago, my sisters and I visited the First National Bank in Fairmont, and visited one of *the Haeckel boys who was now president of the bank. He, too, remembered the happy relationship between the families. This family continued to remember our family throughout the years—deaths and our parents' 50th wedding anniversary. Many of the children are scattered from Martin County, and several of the children have passed away. I could locate that beautiful old home in Fairmont yet today.*

The place was in poor condition, it had been rented out to different ones every year, but it was a good location and fixing it up with care would make a lovely home for us. We had the main house fixed over some, the big rambling porch was torn down and we had an extra room there—a small sun porch. It made a nice warm room. We moved March 1, it was a rainy day. The road was muddy, so traveling was hard. It was a large house, 4 big bedrooms upstairs, besides closets so we enjoyed the house. The first thing we did was to improve the yard. There was no fence, so hogs were living in the yard of the former renters. There was a beautiful lilac tree, the hogs were living under that. When we could work the yard, the men raked and planted grass seed and put a fence around the yard. Soon, grass came and we mowed the lawn. We did little by little and made a place for a garden, and we planted the garden not far from the house. Julane was yet attending normal and would be through in May. Carmen and Woodrow are in Round Lake High School. The rest are in the lower grades. They liked the school and the teachers were very kind to them. I especially remember the kindness that Mr. Lundholm, the Superintendent, showed to this large family those spring days when we enrolled in school and tried to make new friends among strangers—that feeling of being an "outsider" was difficult, and Mr. Lundholm made it easier for all of us. Our dad served on the Round Lake School Board and was a good friend of Mr. Lundholm.

Jerald was busy helping Dad and we had a married man on our other place. Now we needed not board or care for a hired man. The place was beginning to look like home. The house had 6 rooms down. It was a well planned house built so long ago. The rooms were arranged nicely. When school was out, the girls and I were planning how to remodel it. There was a dining room and at the end of the room was a small room used as a pantry. I suppose Carmen took an axe one day and was taking the wall down, and she got quite a way, but we had to get a carpenter and Dad to finish. When we tore the shelves and wall down, it made a lovely long dining room. Then we papered the long room. We were very proud of our work. You would not know the room now. Then we papered the living room the same. So it made a nice room as it was a large opening between the living room and dining room. The boys were busy with the farm work and their 4-H club work. They had livestock baby beefs and hogs. The girls were taking flowers, bread baking, and canning. This would be for the Nobles County Fair. We were now living in Nobles County, 12 miles from Worthington. That was the county seat of Nobles County. Time was going fast. Douglas was 2 years old when we moved here, now he had started to school here. He was 6 years old. He did very well in school, he was quick to learn.

We were now living in our Clover Leaf Stock Farm. Dad took the mailbox along and the name Clover Leaf Stock Farm was still on the box. The girls and I papered some rooms. We papered the dining room and living room the same kind of paper, and we now ate in the kitchen. It was big enough to be used as an eating place, too. Then we could keep our other rooms clean.

The 4-H club project was rather a new organization when our family was growing up, but when they became of age to be members, we had them join. Their dad used to raise purebred Hereford cattle, so the oldest ones joined 4-H club work. It was Jerald, Julane, Woodrow, and Carmen. They all took baby beef calves to feed and raise for the County Fair, which was at Martin County. Now they were kept busy caring for their show calves. They all received prizes for their work at the Martin County Fair. They won a trip to the 4-H club showing at the University Farm School—4-H club week, too. (Junior Livestock Show held in S. St. Paul was Dad's special joy.)

Now a few years had gone by. We had a family of 9—5 sons and 4 girls. We moved to a larger farm of 640 acres, which we bought on a contract—about 2 miles from Round Lake, Nobles County. Julane and Carmen now decided to take Home Improvement as we could not all take baby beef. Lola and Barbara were now old enough to join 4-H club work. We decided to take gardening, canning, sewing and bread baking, and flowers. Julane took canning. In those days, there was no electricity on the farms, so she had to use the wash boiler to cook the vegetables in glass jars, but she won a prize at the County Fair in Nobles, but Carmen took gardening and flowers. Lola took bread baking and won in that. (What a busy place at county fair time, and achievement when we demonstrated and won blue ribbons) Barbara took sewing. She was so good, but she was too young to go to the State Fair. She was the champion sewer of Nobles County. The polio was so bad that fall, too. The girls were all good at Home Improvement, "that they won trips to the livestock show at St. Paul. Barbara was 4-H style queen in one year. She made a suit for the fair and was tops. Gordon had the grand champion calf baby beef at the fair, so did Jerald win in his work. Woodrow, also, did well. He received an honor from the Farm University for his 4-H club work in judging, so he got to attend the farm school at St. Paul where he received his high school diploma as he did not finish at Round Lake school. He was also on the judging team at the farm school. All of the children were in 4-H club work. It was a wonderful organization. It gave them something to do for others and themselves. Cleo Jenkins was our 4-H club leader. She was such a wonderful leader. She resigned and then Mrs. Psorske became our leader.

(At this point in her history, Geneva asked her daughter Carmen to add some material about 4-H. Carmen's addition is in italic.)

Dear Carmen,
I cannot write anymore. Why don't you add a few lines. You were so good in 4-H club work. You helped Lola and Barbara so much.
Love,
Mother

We won trips to the Junior Livestock Show in South St. Paul with our calves and our dad dearly loved those trips to the cities to see his "kids" show off their prize calves—how he taught us to line up the cattle just right so the judges would see only the good side of the calf. It must have worked for we won many prizes at the Junior Livestock Show. How we can recall walking up and down the long lane on the Clover Leaf Stock Farm with our 4-H calves as we prepared them for the Martin County Fair. Dad never missed a Junior Livestock Show. Our mother always went up for just one day—the day of the judging. We were always proud of our parents, they were a well-dressed attractive pair. Dad, also, knew many of the commission men in South St. Paul. Did Dad drive up every day from Granada to South St. Paul? Yes, the Wilson kids were important to the lives of Jake and Geneva.

There would be many interesting tales to tell of our participation in the County Fairs—the prize cattle in the Martin County Fair all lined up with their names on the stalls and every cow had to have a name of Lily. Our father standing around smoking a cigar and visiting with the commission men who had come to bid on the cattle.

We made trips to various parts of the state to purchase the beef cattle for the showing—I particularly recall the McGreger family in Mapleton. We were to notice a round barn near Vernon Center, and THAT ROUND BARN is still on that farm. I also remember attending the Faribault County Fair in Blue Earth.

I bought lots of chickens. I bought 1000 chicks every spring. We sold eggs to the hatchery. The girls would help with the housework while I cared for the baby chicks. It was a pleasant time to go out early and care for the chicks. We had them out on the fields with oil burning heaters for heat for the chicks. I had a big garden and the girls helped me with that. We would get our work done in the morning and in the p.m. we would go somewhere. (The story goes that if the men were working in the fields on the east of the place, the girls and mother would use the west road to get to Worthington, and vice versa.) I never learned to drive. I was too busy and the boys and girls learned to drive and it was easier to get driving licenses then. The boys and girls learned to drive when they were very young. There were no driving lessons taught in the high school like it became later. We did not have electricity on the farm. We used lanterns and lamps and they had to be cleaned and filled every morning. That was a work, just that. The field work was done by horses. We worked lots of land, many acres, 320 acres at first, the threshers were home to be fed, when we threshed our grain there would be at least 20 to 24 men for three to five days of threshing. It took lots of food. When we husked corn we had to feed and keep the men. They husked the corn by hand with wagons and horses. Later years we bought a tractor. That reduced keeping so many hired men and soon the boys could run the tractor so we did not have to board and have an extra man. We also had a car now. Then later we bought a combine. We no longer had to thresh the grain. And, we had no threshing crew to feed. It sure made a difference in the house. After the combine we got a corn husker so we no longer had the corn husking crew to feed.

We had lived on this new place for a few years. We had a big yard to mow and have a lawnmower that we push by hand. Lots of work but we loved to keep the lawn nice. We had planted lots of flowers, every year I would plan rose bushes and peonies. The girls took flowers for 4-H club work and also took sewing for 4-H. Barbara was 4-H club style queen and won a trip to the State Fair. The polio was so severe that Barbara (and many, many others) could not travel to the fair but her winning suit did go.

Julane had finished normal training in Fairmont and now had a school near Rushmore, Minnesota, a rural school. She was lucky to get a school as teachers were plentiful then. It was a lot different than what came later. We were kept busy in the house. Fuel had to be brought in and water carried in from the well. We used a gas engine to run the washing machine and we used a gas iron to iron the clothes. We had big washings, too. We washed twice a week. Electricity was coming to the farms, but we had not got it yet out here. Electricity came to the farms. It sure was a blessing. We bought it for every room. How wonderful it was to just touch the buttons and there was light in every room that you wanted to use, and the big yard light. How wonderful! Now we had an electric washing machine. What a difference that made for the washing. Now it was a pleasure to wash and iron the clothes with an electric iron. There was a small room off from the kitchen. I guess it must have been an old pantry. We made that over into a bathroom. We had a cistern built, so we had water installed in the house. We made our house more modern by getting a septic tank. Now we did not need to carry the water or carry the waste water out. What a difference it made for us in the house, and the men got a milking machine, and the separator was all run by electricity. We also had a sidewalk built of cement around the house from the front gate to the back gate in the yard fence. We also had a bedroom down there that we made into a smaller bedroom and the rest was made into a utility room for washing clothes. I had my machine put in there. It sure made a difference in the work. We had all joined the Methodist Church at Worthington. We know the pastor as he was at Granada and we were members of that church. He moved to Worthington, so when we came to near Worthington, we were members of his church again. The older ones went to Epworth League where they met new friends. We were strangers out here. We missed our friends in Granada, but we soon learned to like new friends, too. Julane taught the Sunday School class for young girls. I myself taught the Women's Bible. It was called the Dorcas class and we had Dorcas class parties every month.

We had been here now a few years, and we enjoyed our home. Carmen had finished high school and was one of the high students. She planned to go to Waldorf College to get a certificate for teaching. She attended Waldorf and received her Iowa certificate for teaching. Julane had been teaching now for a few years in rural schools. In the meantime, she and Byron Coyer got married at Emmetsburg, Iowa, on February 25, 1939. She did not want anyone to know of it as it might have interfered with her teaching, but it did not. They lived with the Coyers until Byron got a house for them to live in by themselves. Byron was a clean young man and a good worker. Julane kept on teaching and Byron farmed with his father. Then, his father became ill, so Byron worked the farm. The Coyers went to Arizona and on trips across the United States. Woodrow was now attending the Agricultural School in St. Paul. He got a scholarship through 4-H club work. He also took high school studies, which he needed as he did not graduate from Round Lake High School, as he got his credits up there. He was on the judging team, so he received honors in this work. We were up to his graduation. Now the Agricultural School joined with the University of Minnesota.

Carmen got a school at Ionia, Iowa, near the Little Brown Church in the Vale. Cook was the Superintendent of the school. They were good people, and Carmen became a favorite of them. They had a baby girl born to them and they named her Carmen.

Lola was in Blue Earth taking normal training for a year. Then she got a country school near Rushmore. She had a hard school. Then, the next year, she taught near Reading. She had a good school and a good place to board, with Mr. and Mrs. Harry Clarke. In the summer, she went to summer school at Mankato, and she also attended the Lutheran Bible School in Minneapolis.

When Lola was about 12 years old, she fell from a swing and broke her arm at the shoulder and also fractured the bone. We could not find any doctor that could replace and mend the shoulder. We took her to the doctor at Ocheyedan, Iowa. There was not much of a hospital here in Worthington at that time. The doctor at Ocheyedan advised us to take her to the University Hospital in Minneapolis, which we did. She was up there for about six weeks. Then we went for her. Now we thought that we would have a big bill to pay for her being there so long, but she was put in a 12 year old children's ward, which a lady had put money for children of that age. It was no cost for them. We did not have to pay one cent, and she had such wonderful care. We were very thankful that Lola recovered so well, and also thankful for the lady who donated so much money to that ward. We were thankful for the doctors and nurses who took such good care of her.

Later on, when she had taught country school and saved up some money, she went to Mankato College to get her Minnesota Teacher's Certificate to teach school in town. Country schools were now being consolidated. She got a school at Ocheyedan, for which we were thankful, and she was too. She taught there for a few years.

Barbara was now in high school. She was one of the highest. I remember I wrote her speech for her, which she gave on graduation night. She would now attend Waldorf for 2 years. Then she got a school at Lake Park, Iowa, which she taught for a few years until she was married, and some years after she was married. Gordon was working on our farm and so were Jerald and Sanford. They were all kept busy. They had all finished high school, except Douglas. He was the youngest.

Carmen was now teaching at Lakota, Iowa—that was closer. The Cooks went to Lakota from Ionia and Carmen went, too, to be a teacher there. She had been attending Mankato College in the summer to get her Minnesota Teacher's Certificate. She met a young farmer boy, Kenneth Jones. She became engaged to him. He was a nice boy, good, clean young man. She was married on August 6, 1944 at the Methodist church in Worthington. Dr. Lillico was the pastor and Julane was the bridesmaid. We had a small reception. We were busy at this time before the wedding. We were threshing. We had not gotten our combine yet and we were putting in electricity. We would miss Carmen, but she would have a good home and a good husband.

Douglas had finished high school. He was one of the top graduates. He went to Minnesota Bible College where he studied to be a minister. He worked some extra to get some money. Later, he was assistant pastor here in Worthington. When he was attending Minnesota Bible College, he had a small church—Eagle Lake, Minnesota. He graduated from Minnesota Bible College. Then he got a church at St. Francisville in S.E. Illinois, and he went to Lincoln Bible College while he was pastor there. We went down to see him. It was a wonderful trip down there. We attended his church and also drove to Kentucky and through Indiana. We traveled a lot now, when there were no children at home. They were all grown.

In the meantime, the World War broke out. How well I remember that day. How awful that war was. All able bodied boys had to be enlisted, and they had to go to war. We had 4 sons who were of age to go. Jerald was the oldest, so he had to go first. He was in good health, and his I.Q. was high.

We took him to the train. What a day! I will never forget seeing my son go to war, and coming home was worse, to see his empty bed and all his clothes hanging in the closet. He had a good girl friend, Lenore Sampson. She was a teacher in Lake Park, Iowa. Woodrow was home now, after graduating from the St. Paul Agricultural School. He also received his high school credits there as he did not finish high school in Round Lake. Woodrow was drafted a few weeks later. We took him to the train. It was a rainy day, and it was so sad to have another son go to war. We missed the 2 boys very much. Jerald had a pet dog. We found him dead one day. I think he was lonesome for Jerald. Gordon was now our helper. Sanford was home, too, but he wanted to enlist in the army. We kept a married man in our other place. We worked 640 acres besides hogs, feeding cattle, and milk cows, so we needed the help. Woodrow was shipped to England where he worked in the hospital. He was in the Medical Corps. We were so glad he was not in the infantry. Jerald was in Fort Ord, then he was sent to New Guinea or the island near the Philippines. He was also in the Medical Division. He drove the ambulances and helped in the hospital there. They never said much about it, but when the war was over, they both came home safely. We were thankful. Now Stanford joined up for the army. He wanted to be a paratrooper, which he joined up for. He became a paratrooper, but he found out jumping from the plane was not easy, and every jump did not lessen the fear of jumping. He paratrooped in Germany, but the war was about over then. He arrived home safely after the war.

Jerald helped Dad with the work on the farm. He had Lenore, so he was happy to be back. Woodrow was not so satisfied on the farm. He wanted to go back to school, so he enrolled in the Minnesota Lutheran Bible School (LBI). He became interested in religion. He decided he wanted to become a Lutheran minister. Different people advised him to become a minister. He became acquainted with a nurse who was attending LBI. They became engaged. She was from Volga, South Dakota. Her name was Dora Starkenberg. She was a lovely girl. They were married, and then Woodrow attended Lutheran Seminary to study for the ministry. Woodrow attended school in the day, and Dora worked at nights, and Woodrow worked some, too. They had to make a living, too. They lost two of their first children, but later on, they had a son who they named Warren. One of the children which they had lost was a still born baby girl named Nancy. She was buried in the Worthington cemetery where the place for infants was. If she had lived, she would be a grown young lady. Her burial was August 20, 1948. There was no funeral services. Woodrow came with the body and left it there overnight. I can still remember it. How sad it was. We went with Woodrow to the burial place. Then he went back to school. Dora was not able to come.

Lola was teaching in Ocheyedan public school. She became engaged to a nice young man from Worthington. He worked for the gas company Natural Gas. She received a diamond and was married August 20, 1950. He was a very nice young man. His father was Chief of Police here in Worthington. We were happy for them. They were married on a Sunday, in the M.E. church. Barbara was the bridesmaid. It was small, but a very nice little wedding. They were a lovely couple. Lola kept on teaching. They got an apartment and Bob drove to Worthington to work. Barbara graduated from Waldorf College. She could now teach in Iowa. She got a school at Lake Park, Iowa, not far from home. She taught there a few years. We used to get her Friday p.m. and take her back on Sunday p.m. On Saturday, we would go someplace, Sioux Falls or Spencer. We had a good time. Gordon was the main help while the boys were at war. He became interested in the nurses at the Worthington Hospital. He became acquainted with one, Delores Nord. She was a lovely person and a wonderful nurse.

We had now remodeled our rooms downstairs. We put in big windows in the rooms. A large window in the dining room and 2 big windows in the living room. You would not know the rooms. We took the old windows out and put those big new ones in. Then I painted the windows and got a lady to paper the 2 rooms, and I got drapes made for the 3 big windows. Then we carpeted the 2 rooms. They really looked nice. We took the bedroom and made a smaller one. It was big enough for a single bed, and the rest was a utility room where I washed clothes. We put in a good furnace to heat the upstairs, too. We used the upstairs for our sleeping rooms. Then we went to work on our kitchen. We tore all the old cupboards down and put new ones up, and also put a nice big window over our new sink. We put in a new floor and new linoleum. Now we thought that we had a new kitchen, too. I stained and varnished the cupboards. We had a carpenter do all the work. Now we could entertain the 4-H clubs and young people. I belonged to the Methodist circles, also the Dorcas class, Mother's Service Club from Worthington. I would entertain them. They seemed to like to come out in the country. We had lived here now a few years, and had had good crops and good livestock. We were now over the Depression and the children were pretty well grown up. Dad and I went on trips. We really enjoyed our home and family. Every Christmas, we would have the family

Christmas party on Christmas Day night. We always had oyster stew on Christmas Eve. Douglas was in Illinois, now going to school. We were down to see him. Enoch and Myrtle Sampson went with us once. He had a small country church near Paris, Illinois, and he taught school in a Paris consolidated school. It was a nice room. He was going with a good young girl. Her name was Karen McKinney. They became engaged. Her folks came to visit us. Doug and Karen had come a few days before. They went to Sioux Falls to visit some people. When we went to visit Doug at Paris, Illinois, we visited Lincoln's places where he worked. It was interesting to visit these places. We stayed at the best motels and ate at the best cafes. We had some wonderful trips. We had a new Lincoln car, so we sure enjoyed our trips.

From a collection of themes written by Catha Jones for an English class, January 20, 1960.

My Grandfather

My grandpa is seventy-five years old, but still he loves to drive his big Lincoln. Ever since he was thirty-five years old, he has thought he could drive with just a chauffeur's license, but he found out that you needed more than that, when a policeman stopped him about five years ago. He is a brave driver, but once he lost his courage. He was driving to Indianapolis, Indiana to visit his son at the University. But in spite of his braveness, he could not drive to the college campus because he didn't have enough nerve. His son came by taxi to where Grandpa was, and he drove the car to the campus. So this shows with my grandfather, that age makes no difference in what you can enjoy doing. My grandfather is seventy-five years old. Even though he is quite old, he does not act his age. He still runs his own farm and raises two hundred head of beef cattle, and he would hate to give it up. He loves to travel and he drives his own car. Every year, he takes a trip, not a distant trip, but he goes wherever he wishes to go. For his hobby, he plays the violin. He is a very good player, and he plays in a small orchestra in Worthington. Even though by grandfather looks his age, he does not like to act seventy-five years old.

Douglas and Karen were married June 1, 1962. We went to the wedding. The wedding was small. Karen and Doug went to Tennessee for their hone moon. Doug got a job as the Pastor in the Church of Christ Church in

Pipestone (Minnesota.) They could not afford a full-time minister therefore, Dc got a teaching job in Lake Benton. Karen and Doug got a nice home. It was a cottage with a living room, dining area, bedroom and closet-like back kitchen and hall. It was a dandy new home. They liked it fine. They stayed there two years, we visited them often, but Douglas was not satisfied and wanted to go back to school for another degree.

Carmen and Kenneth moved to a farm not far from Cambria, Minnesota. He farmed with his brother (Ed) who lived on the Jones' home farm place. Carmen and Ken have had three children: Kent Wilson Jones born in New on June 2, 1947; Catha Jean Jones born in New Ulm on September 2, 1948 (Catha was just like an angel here on this earth. She became ill with leu and passed away June 29, 1974. It was a sad death but she is with her K without any more pain or suffering. We were all saddened by her death. was such a lovely girl, so kind and thoughtful of everyone she knew. I could not go and see her when she was ill or attend her funeral. I was too ill.) Janeva Ann Jones was born in New Ulm on June 28, 1954.

Barbara is now teaching in Lake Park, Iowa. She met a good, you farmer. They kept going together for a few years. Then they were married in the ME Church by Dr. Leach on May 1, 1953. Barbara kept teaching as they were married. They lived on the Burnside home farm place about four miles south of Lake Park. They had a son, Carter, born on January 19, 1960. After Carter was a little older, Barbara went back to teaching. After a few years they rented their land out and moved to Sioux City, Iowa. They bought a lovely new home. Barbara went back to teaching near Sioux City, Iowa. She had some distance to drive. Later on, she got a school in Sioux City, and Carter was attending school in Sioux City. I am writing this in 1976, and he is now a young man. He took violin lessons and played in the Sioux City Junior orchestra. He played well on his violin. Both of his grandfathers played the violin.

Now in 1976, Douglas and Karen live at Brooklyn, Iowa. He is principal there. It is a consolidated school, so he is kept busy. They have bought a lovely new home and have 2 children. Bethany is now a first grader, and Phil is 4 and a half years old.

Gordon had been home helping on the farm and doing very well. He became interested in a nurse at the Worthington Hospital. She was from Iona and was a lovely person. They became engaged. We were happy for Gordon to have such a wonderful person to become his wife. They were married October 18, 1947 in Iona Lutheran Church. They had a lovely wedding. They went to Niagara Falls on their honeymoon.

We bought a small house for them. It was a good newly built house. It had 3 rooms. It was small, but good. Dolores kept on nursing at the hospital. They had a son later on, they named him Steve. He was a cute little fellow. Nords, Dolores's folks, came down to our place, and we had built a new room to their house. Then we had a cistern made for them. Before, they had to carry all their washing clothes water from our place. Their home was placed in a yard by themselves. Then we had a basement built, so we had their house moved over on the new basement. When we had the cistern dug, Steve fell into the cistern. Dolores did some nursing. Then Steve came over and I took care of him when Dolores worked. Gordon bought part of our farm. Dolores fixed up the little house so pretty. They lived there a few years, then Gordon bought a farm close to ours and they moved over there. Dolores got sick with cancer, but she recovered from one operation fairly well for 10 years. They had 5 children: Steve, Sharon, Randall Lee, Bruce, and Keith. When Dolores improved in health, they remodeled their house so they had a beautiful place. Dolores suffered so, the last year of her life. We all loved her, she was an angel. She passed away at the Regional Hospital on October 2, 1971. She was buried at Round Lake Cemetery. The funeral was October 4. How we all missed her.

Jerald and Lenore bought some of our farm. They lived on the place where we had for hired people. Jerald and Dad had turkeys, but later on, they dissolved being together, so Jerald had turkeys of his own. The price was good for a few years, but later on, the price was low, so he went more dairy and hog raising. On the place were very few trees. Jerald planted so many trees. Now he had a good big house and so many trees, you would not have known the place. They had 4 children.

Now at this time of writing—February 17, 1976, they have all finished high school and are married. Edith had 2 children, Jeanne had 2—Mary has none and John was just married on November 29, 1975. They also went to Junior College. They are a lovely family. Jeanne taught school at Lamberton, Minnesota. There is where she met her husband, Ronald Kelsey. They have a beautiful home. Mary became a nurse, and she is married now. They live in Maryland. They are a lovely family. Jerald and Lenore are alone now. Their place is so nice, a lovely bunch of trees and evergreens. Gordon had fixed up his place so nice, too. He was a good farmer.

Gordon remarried. It was hard to be left alone. The family was all home, but Dolores lived to see Steve and Janet get married. Sharon was married too, later. She stayed with me when she went to Junior College, before her marriage. I lived in Inn Towne Apartments then. She was a lovely person. Gordon got a good wife. She had taught in Round Lake for 20 years, but when they were married, she had taught some other school near Mankato. Gordon had a lovely family. He and his wife were living in Round Lake where Gordon worked at buying and selling homes. He also had the school bus to drive. Randy and his wife were living on Gordon's farm. Bruce was going to the University in St. Paul, and Keith was a senior in high school.

Stanford was a doctor (V.E.M.). He was now in Preston, Minnesota. They had 8 children. Sandy graduated from a musical college in New Mexico. Two girls were married, Susan and Nancy. They were lovely girls, and have good homes. Chuck was in the air force. They had twin boys, about 11 years now. They were David and Thomas and little Kristan. She was very talented—well they were all very talented. Stanford had bulbar polio while he was going to school. They had 2 children, and he had to support his family besides going to school. It was with God's help that he recovered from the terrible sickness. They were living in St. Paul then, and Stan was going to school at the University, but he graduated and got work at Storm Lake, Iowa first.

Lola had 3 children. She had been teaching and going to school to get her degree. She had a good husband and a lovely home. They now live in Worthington and she is teaching there. Time had gone by fast. Her two girls would be married this summer. They were now in college. Lola's husband was the manager of the big Natural Gas Company here and other Natural Gas Companies in other towns in this territory of the Northwest.

Barbara and Dale and their son Carter live in Myers Court, Sioux City, Iowa. She lived there. They had rented their farms and Dale was in the real estate business. Carter played the violin and was in the school orchestra. He is now about 16 years of age. He was a good player on the violin. His 2 grandfathers played the violin. It seemed to be easy for him.

Douglas and Karen lived in Brooklyn. He was principal of the school there. They had 2 children. Bethany would be in the second grade and Phil would be in kindergarten this coming fall. How the time does go by.

It is now the year of February 23, 1976.

After Douglas and Karen's marriage in the year of June 1, 1962, all the family was married and gone from home. Our farm home was all modern now and we enjoyed our home. We now had plenty of time. Jerald lived not far from us, about one half mile, so we saw them nearly every day. We went to church regularly. I taught a class in the Methodist church. Now I'm in the year of 1962. We went to visit Doug and Karen when they were married. After the children were married, Dad and I had plenty of time. We traveled a lot to Sioux City, Sioux Falls, and down to Texas where Barbara and Dale lived. Dale was there in the army. They came back to their farm when the war was over. We had a Study Club in Round Lake for a few years. I enjoyed that. I now had plenty of time after my big family had grown up. Then we started a Home Project group. It was in Round Lake. I was elected one of the leaders. There was only 1 group in Indian Lake Township. Later on, I was elected chairman of Indian Lake. I organized 6 project groups. We learned to do so many things. It was real interesting. The County Home Demonstration agent was our leader for Nobles County. Her name was Dorothy Bessimore. She was also leader for 4-H work. She was good to help the girls with their 4-H club, like sewing. Dorothy Bessimore said that I had worked so hard helping to organize these new project groups in our Indian Lake Township, that I should be given a trip to the Farm Bureau Short Course, which is held every September at the University Farm. The University Farm was part of the Minnesota State University at St. Paul. It was wonderful to attend those Farm Bureau Programs. We stayed at the girl's dormitory. It was before the school started. We had our meals at the cafeteria or eating places. It was very good. There were quite a few who went from Nobles County. It was for the Minnesota Farm Bureau Women. They were from all over Minnesota. Good speakers and crafts were taught. I learned how to chip carve on bass wood plates. We drew our designs. The plates were soft wood and we used single edge razor blades. I kept up this hobby until I could enjoy it. We attended the meetings every year for a number of years. Then we had to meet at Lake Koronis, Paynesville, Minnesota, as the farm school was united with the state university, but the camp at Lake Koronis was more of a camp. It had family style eating, and we had to sleep more in each room, but we had a wonderful time. Good programs all day, and also in the evenings. It was beautiful up there near the big lake. I attended the Women's Farm Bureau for 20 years, but my hearing was getting worse, so I had to quit the project meeting as leader and chairman, but I sure enjoyed the work, but I kept up my hobbies, such as chip carving and I carved many plates. I took them to the Nobles County Fair and would receive first prize. I sold some, and gave away many as gifts. That was years ago, but now I see my plates, and I cannot do that anymore, as I am in a rest home and am 86 years of age when I am writing these pages. My big family had all married and had homes of their own and had families.

My husband and I lived on the farm after our children were married. We had a big farm—640 acres and we bought 80 more, so we had 720 acres. Jerald bought 160 acres, and Gordon bought 400 acres, so we had 160 acres which we lived on. My husband was not able to farm alone, so he hired help. We had one man who worked for us for 20 years. He was married and lived in Round Lake. I gave him his dinner and sometimes lunches in busy seasons, but our place was now modern, so it was pleasant out on the farm. We had a new Lincoln car. We traveled a lot. When Woodrow was going to school to be a minister, he was county agent in the summer at Park Rapids, Minnesota. We went up to visit him while he was working there. It was a beautiful park up there. He had a home, but we stayed in the camp building. We did our own cooking. We enjoyed it a lot. It was beautiful up there in the summer, and also a lovely drive up there. We went to Duluth and other places while up there. He finished his training for a Lutheran pastor » and his first church was at Albion, Nebraska, west of Sioux City. It was in the hilly country, but a beautiful parsonage. His next place was Clark, South Dakota. He was there 7 years. Warren was the oldest son. Then they were blessed with 3 more children. We went to visit him while he was at Clark South Dakota. It was a lovely trip up there. They had a lovely new church and a beautiful parsonage. Now he is in Geneva, Nebraska. They have been there 7 years, and their 3 oldest are in the University in Lincoln, Nebraska. Warren had graduated from college and so had Tracy. He had a wonderful family. Tristi, too, had about finished. His wife Dora had been working some, too. She was a nurse. We had been to visit them, too. We were still on the farm, but we had bought a home in Worthington, Minnesota, and also a home in Round Lake in case we wanted to move. Now I had more time on my hands. I had worked many cross stitch pictures, and had given them to the families. I also made myself 3 crochet suits. One was yellow, one was rose pink, and the last one was teal blue. They were crocheted in good yarn.

On June 14, 1964, we celebrated our golden wedding day—50 years. It was held at the United Methodist Church in Worthington. The family helped and also my circle that I belonged to. Woodrow gave the program. He was the pastor then, at Clark, South Dakota. All the family was home for it. It was a big day, and many people came. It was the biggest crowd that the church had ever had, so they said. We received many beautiful cards, and it was lovely. We were very thankful for our many friends, and all of our families. It was held in the old M.E. church. It was before we built this big new church, but the old church was beautiful, too. We were very grateful for the lovely golden anniversary that was held June 14, 1964. We would always remember that day. We were kept busy on the farm. Julane was teaching and was principal in Round Lake School. Carmen had bought a lovely home in Windom and was teaching there. Ken works at the Post Office. He rented his farm out, and the building to another party. They had Janeva. She now went to Oral Roberts University and liked it fine. Janeva had also graduated from Waldorf College. Jerald was busy farming. He had bought the east 160 acres of our farm. There were no trees on the place, but now it was a wonderful grove. He had been planting trees every year, so it was just lovely. He had lived there now nearly 30 years, so a big grove had grown, too. Julane and Byron had built a lovely home on the east side of Indian Lake. She still teaches. They had one son, Brian, and he had gone to Macalester College, and was also in India to study. We sold more land to Gordon, so we had now 160 acres left. We were farming that with Carney Knutson's help. We bought a home in Round Lake. It was from one of the teacher's homes. We were now getting up in years, so we could not work like we used to.

So ends Mother's side of the story. As each year went by, it became a bit more difficult for her to put the words together. [The rest of the text is from Carmen and other family members.]

In the spring of 1968, our parents sold the family farm to John Vihlen. John was a young farmer from Indian Lake Township who had always admired our place and had earlier indicated a desire to purchase the Wilson farm. After purchasing a new Buick, Mother and Dad moved into their Round Lake home. On May 27, Dad passed away from a massive heart attack at the Worthington Hospital. The funeral services were held at the Worthington Methodist Church, on May 29, with burial at the Worthington cemetery. The church was filled to capacity with friends and family. Neighbors and hired men from the Fairmont and Granada communities came to pay their last respect to a beloved friend, as well as many acquaintances from Nobles County. Jake had served on the Round Lake School Board for 15 years, had been active in Farm Bureau work, and played the violin in the Worthington Civic Community Orchestra. He will be remembered as playing in the "Messiah" for Christmas concerts. His outgoing personality and friendly handshake will always be missed. He always took time for a cup of coffee and a piece of pie. As Reverend Ireland told the family on that beautiful day in May, "Can't you hear the angels in Glory Rejoicing Jake Wilson has arrived?"

After Dad's death, Mother sold her Round Lake home and moved to the Inn Towne Apartments in Worthington. She had a lovely place to live, and was able to walk to church and downtown to do her shopping and made frequent visits to the library. She continued to be active with her Bible studies and coffee parties until her accident in December 1973. On a December day, she and Henry Sampson were driving to Round Lake, and she was injured as the car hit an icy spot in the road. Mr. Sampson passed away. Mother was hospitalized in Sioux Falls for some time, and in the spring of 1974, became a resident of the Fauskee Rest Home in Worthington. She accepted this role in a positive way, and was cheerful in spite of a voice and a hearing loss. She was able to write notes to us, and to visit our homes, and go to the local cafes frequently. Her cheerful attitude carried her during these days, as she made friends in the home—and occupied a special chair in the lobby. It seemed to be her philosophy to try to find ONLY the good in situations; such as a time when the food at the nursing home was very bland and uninteresting, she wrote: We had boiled cabbage for dinner, BUT the bread and coffee were good. Our mother passed away December 2, 1980. The funeral was a tribute to a faithful Christian. Pastor Nelson reflected on a life of dedication to a living Lord and her loyalty to her family and the church.

Since it is my responsibility to complete the life of Geneva, I have gleaned precious moments from family members:

I remember mostly how tirelessly she worked to keep us feeling good and nutritionally sound, always to be sure that we had clean milk and sanitary food. One day when the family was short of milk, she sent a young son into the pasture to milk one of the cows. Mother always tried to be fair to each of us. We had our turns sitting on her lap. She never wavered in her faith even though times were often difficult. She valued an education—books, trips to the library, and music lessons for the daughters, 4-H clubs for ALL the children.

"Mother"

My very first memory of my family was that it was a bright and sunny winter morning, and that it was a very special day, a holiday or Sunday. Anyway, a lot of activity was bustling around there as a new baby sister had arrived. One of the most amusing incidents occurred on a late afternoon on a hot summer day. All the family would go swimming in one of the chain of lakes near Fairmont. Mother being a modest person, found it hard and the older children, hilarious, to try to get Mother to go into the water, something she had never done before and MAYBE never since, for swimming was not her thing. Her two older daughters pushed her in the water and splashed water on her. It was fun for everyone but MOTHER. Mostly though, life was serious for our mother—in the thirties. Raising 9 children was not an amusing thing, and it was serious business for Geneva.

We can recall a kind father who tried to take time for his children, bringing us candy treats from town, and buying ice cream cones on Saturday night. When we would see the car coming down the long lane, we would run out to meet him, and be given a ride home with a loving father. There were many short trips about the countryside. One can still see the map of Minnesota on the desk with county seats clearly marked. One particular trip was to view a round barn near Vernon Center, THAT barn still stands as a landmark today, and the boulevards in New Ulm. We often attended the Faribault County Fair in Blue Earth. While living in Martin County, our father would show prize beef cattle and horses. The two older brothers were left at home one Sunday afternoon to groom a horse for the races. The horse was put through obstacle courses, and during one of the practices, one of the brothers got tangled in a barbed wire fence, the other brother hastily poured a bottle of iodine over the open wound—indeed, a quick trip to the Fairmont Hospital when the parents arrived home. It seems that iodine and kerosene were our medicines in those long ago days.

Our parents liked to drive around the countryside, it was said that neighbors in Indian Lake Township could set their clocks at four o'clock when the Wilson's left for Worthington for their afternoon lunch. We were, also, raised in a family with disciplines and were taught that some practices were wrong and others right. In the early thirties, we had a hired man—Melvin Flatten—from northern Minnesota. It was his practice to go into

Granada every Saturday night and spend his wages at the local tavern. One evening he came back to our farm quite inebriated, so the two older sisters thought they would teach him a lesson. They locked their bedroom door, put chairs under the knob, and sang the old hymns of the Methodist church as loudly as they dared, hoping that he would hear and convert his ways. There were many hired men, and their families whom our father helped through the years. Also, I remember our mother fixing Christmas packages for many needy families in Granada.

Our family showed much love toward each other. When Mother went to the Fairmont Hospital with her eighth child, the children at home were responsible for the care of the younger ones, and the household. But we can recall going to the hospital to see our mother and picking a bouquet of wild roses to bring to Mother—they were wrinkled by the time we arrived, but our father had seen to it that we could stop along the dusty road and pick a bouquet of wild roses.

Let us remember a kind and loving father. He was concerned for his family. We can recall how he helped his two sisters and brother providing jobs and homes for them when in need. Jake was born November 21, 1885 near Roland, Iowa. He lived in Omaha, Nebraska until his mother's death around 1890. Then his father left the family, and Jake was raised by his grandparents near Roland. Sam Wilson went west, joined the gold rush, did a variety of jobs, especially working in a Danish college, Solvang, California, where he died and is buried. He did not see his family for almost twenty years, but he came back and spent summers with us. He was fortunate in having a forgiving family. Dad helped his sister Helen raise her children, he helped Aunt Mattie and Uncle Matt find jobs throughout the years. They were employed as a hired man on a farm near Truman, Minnesota. Their son Waldo Johnson still resides in Truman, Minnesota. Uncle Julius, Dad's brother, and his wife Sadie, spent many summers with us, as Uncle Julius was a carpenter and repaired buildings and helped build a livestock barn for the Clover Leaf Stock Farm. Aunt Sadie was a beautiful lady and spent many hours with her "make-up" and pretty clothes. They had no children, and we loved to watch Aunt Sadie.

Dad was, also, an encourager. When our mother began to become interested in crafts when the children had gone from home, he saw to it that she was able to shop for what she needed, and participate in the fairs and many organizations. He encouraged her to dress well. He was proud of his Geneva.

"My Parents Took Time"

ONE OF MOTHER'S FAVORITE BIBLE verses was Ecclesiastes 3:1 - 9—"For everything there is a season, and time for every matter under heaven: a time to be born and a time to die; a time to plant, and a time to pluck up what is planted . . ." So, when I think of my parents, I think of all that they took time to do in their busy lives. My father took time to practice and play the violin. My mother took time to study the Bible and she took time to tell me Bible stories when I was very young. She also took time to teach a Bible class. We took time to laugh and share jokes with one another and we told our jokes to company. One of our favorite jokes was this one:

> "Once there was a mountaineer and his wife. They did not see many people. One day when the man was out walking, he found a mirror. He got very excited. 'Oh, I never knew my pappy had his picture took!' He took the mirror home and hid it. But every day he would sneak away and look at his 'Pappy's picture.' He did this when he thought his wife was not looking. His wife became curious. So one day when her husband was gone, she searched until she found the mirror. 'Oh,' she exclaimed, 'so this is the old hag he's been chasing after.'"

The summer before I entered fifth grade our annual 4-H club tour ended at Psorskes with a picnic and a meeting. For roll call each member was to tell a favorite joke. So I stood up (when my turn came) and said, "The worms were digging in Earnest. Poor Earnest!" No one laughed! And when I sat down I thought of how, at home, the whole family would laugh at this joke. And I thought to myself, "Isn't this funny?"

I can think of so many things that my parents took time to do, in their busy productive lives, during depression and war years, three sons in the service, raising and caring for nine children. Life was not always easy. Yet, I like to remember, "And they also took time to laugh."

From a Granddaughter

By Sharon Wilson Anderson, who lived with Grandma while she attended Worthington Junior College.

When I think of Grandma and Grandpa Wilson, I think of the feeling of their home which was warmth and love. More specifically with Grandpa, of course was his music — his violin. Also, as young children, we thought it was fun to go for a ride in his big fancy cars and he even let us play with his electric windows!

With Grandma I remember the fragrant smells of her great homemade breads, her pies (which were the best), and the smell of her famous egg coffee. As a young girl, I remember her helping me make dolls from her lowers. I also remember the huge family gatherings — in particular — Christmas with all the children and grandchildren gathered at their farmhouse. Grandma many times would crochet something for each of her granddaughters. Her caring and concern for all of her many offspring — no matter how near or far they lived, was always there. Her many letters showed her unselfish love for all those around her and she spoke often of her strong faith. She truly lived her faith in our Lord and she trusted in His love and His plan for her life. I feel fortunate to have had her as my grandmother.

This article appeared in the Methodist Church (Worthington, MN) publication in a series of articles recognizing their senior citizens.

Mrs. Geneva Wilson has always been an avid Bible student. Her children can remember her sitting in the sunporch studying the Bible and underlining favorite passages of scripture. In spite of being a busy farm wife and mother of nine children, she nonetheless found time for daily devotionals and many activities in the church. Whenever the various members of the family would come from college, the *Upper Room* and the Bible were on the kitchen table open to the page for the day. The children learned at an early age her favorite scripture: John 14: 1-3.

In 1935 the Wilson family moved from the community of Granada, Mn. to the Round Lake area. The Wilsons were members of the Granada Methodist Church, now friends and family were curious if they could continue their membership in a Methodist church with Worthington being a ten-mile drive from their farm. However, God was watching over this large family for that same year, Rev. Groenig was transferred from the Granada church to the Worthington Methodist Church. He was overjoyed to know that one of his best Bible teachers was nearby. He visited the family inviting them to church and asking Mrs. Wilson to teach the adult Bible class. She accepted and continued in the role for 30 years as well as other responsible areas of the church. She, also, encouraged her family to become active participants. She considered this assignment a privilege and one has many vivid memories of Mrs. Wilson walking down the aisle of the old Methodist Church carrying her Bible and notebook in hand, elegantly dressed and with a picturesque hat.